GREAT
GRILLED CHEESE

50 Innovative Recipes for Stovetop, Grill, and Sandwich Maker

Laura Werlin

PHOTOGRAPHS BY MAREN CARUSO

Stewart, Tabori & Chang
New York

TO MY SISTER ANDI

• • •

Published in 2004 by
Stewart, Tabori & Chang
An imprint of ABRAMS

Text copyright © 2004 Laura Werlin

Photographs copyright © 2004 Maren Caruso

Library of Congress Cataloging-in-Publication Data
Werlin, Laura.
    Great grilled cheese : 50 innovative recipes for stovetop, grill, and sandwich
    maker / Laura Werlin ; photographs by Maren Caruso.
        p.   cm.
    Includes index.
    ISBN-13: 978-1-58479-338-0
    ISBN-10: 1-58479-338-4
    Cookery (Cheese) 2. Sandwiches I. Title
TXT759.5.C48W47 2004
641.8'4—dc22   2004048108

Editor: Julie Stillman

Designer: Laura Lindgren

The text of this book was composed in Humanist Slabserif and DIN Mittelschrift.

Printed and bound in China
10 9

ABRAMS
THE ART OF BOOKS SINCE 1949
115 West 18th Street
New York, NY 10011
www.abramsbooks.com

CONTENTS

ACKNOWLEDGMENTS

Oh, the joys of writing a cookbook, especially one as fun and as comforting as this one. I have many people to thank for helping bring this project to fruition. Thanks to: Carole Bidnick for being my trusted agent and amazing friend; my editor, Julie Stillman, who has edited all three of my books, thereby deserving a medal; the people at Stewart, Tabori & Chang, especially president and publisher Leslie Stoker, who is equal parts publisher and friend.

To my recipe tester, Annette Flores, whose palate, organizational skills, and work ethic brought good grilled cheese to great. To my friends and family who lent their recipe-testing skills: Cheryl Gould, Suzy Sharp, Richard Stern, and Mom, Dad, and my sister, Andi, who are as loyal as the day is long, and more loving than any people I know.

The creative folks behind this project deserve up-front recognition. Photographer Maren Caruso and the food styling team, Erin Quon and Kim Konecny of EK Foods, embraced the subject of grilled cheese and brought it to life through beautiful pictures; and Laura Lindgren captured the fun and whimsy of grilled cheese in her creative design.

To the many others who have helped along the way: Barbara Cushman who always stands by at the cheese counter at The Pasta Shop in Oakland waiting to hand me a sample of the latest and greatest cheese; Lori Lyn Narlock, a great friend and consistent booster in every way; Lisa Ekus, Dana Whitaker, Diane Tegmeyer, and my foodwriting group, John Birdsall, Linda Carucci, Randy Milden, Jennie Schacht, Elizabeth Thomas, and Thy Tran, who slogged through the first version of the introduction and helped whip it—and me—into shape. I thank you all from the bottom of my heart.

INTRODUCTION

I can't remember a time when I didn't love grilled cheese. As a child, I instinctively appreciated any justification for slathering butter on two slices of sandwich bread, uniting them with gobs of cheese, and then frying the whole thing to a delicate crunch. Sometimes, cheese would escape the clutches of the bread and transform into golden toasty bits in the hot pan. I would immediately scrape them up and pop them in my mouth. And grilled cheese gave me the implicit okay to play with my food, stretching the strands of melted cheese between my front teeth and the sandwich as I pulled it as far from my mouth as my small arms would reach. My fingertips slick with butter, I savored every last lick. Wash my hands? You've got to be kidding.

But as I got older, the allure of the grilled cheese sandwich got even stronger. It made the case for eating slowly and deliberately because the filaments of melted cheese could not be chewed quickly. Their springy nature demanded a slow, thoughtful chew, the kind that, say, saltwater taffy or caramel command. Like those confections, the cheesy strands offered an unparalleled textural satisfaction. And the yin to the pillowy cheese's yang was the crunchy bread that encased it.

For me, the grilled cheese sandwich was never ordinary. It was always a special treat. Melted cheese of any kind was so deeply satisfying that I couldn't imagine a grilled cheese sandwich as something that should be eaten fast or relegated to side status as, say, an accompaniment to tomato soup. Yet that was and is the appeal of grilled cheese. It's a simple food. It's diner food. It's kid food. It's Saturday lunch fare on a chilly day. Occasionally it's even on the menu of a white tablecloth restaurant. It can go anywhere, and it never disappoints.

Versatility is perhaps the grilled cheese sandwich's greatest feature. It can be gussied up when adorned with sautéed rosemary and grapes, or dressed down when paired with a piece of ham, but its core components—melted cheese and bread—always remain the same.

The grilled cheese sandwich also finds its place at a party. Small squares of sourdough-encrusted melted cheddar cheese layered with thin slices of apple and ham can incite a small riot. Sautéed buttery figs nestled in creamy blue cheese will bring a highbrow group to its knees. And those avoiding bread will clamor for the portobello mushroom that houses gooey provolone and an herbed tomato slice. In all these cases, the grilled cheese sandwich shows itself for all that it is—a symbol of infinite possibilities.

Confining those possibilities to just fifty recipes wasn't easy. As I shopped at the market, every produce item suddenly became a potential ingredient; every condiment, the perfect addition; each spice, a door to a world of flavors. And you too should feel free to embellish your grilled cheese however you like.

The sandwich we call "grilled cheese" shows off its adaptability in more than just the ingredients it can showcase. It is also a sandwich that can be cooked in several ways. Despite its name, the *grilled* cheese sandwich as we know it did not begin on a grill. In fact, it may never have been intended for the object we call a grill (see the Grilled Cheese History section that follows). That's why almost every recipe in this book contains instructions for cooking the sandwiches on the stove, in a sandwich maker, or, in their literal form—on the outdoor grill. If you're feeling daring, you can go beyond these three cooking methods and use your broiler or perhaps your oven. Think of these recipes as templates to be filled in with your imagination.

The recipes are centered on the most enticing ways to put bread and cheese together. In addition to recipes for classic grilled cheese sandwiches, you will find recipes that include fruits and vegetables, herbs and spices, meat and fish, even chocolate! And with the soaring popularity of tortillas in this country, I thought it fitting to include five delicious quesadilla recipes. After all, it doesn't get much better than melted cheese encased in a crispy tortilla.

Perhaps it is all these variations—and the possibility of so many more—that have captivated me and drawn me into the world of grilled cheese. I hope that if you are new to this expanded universe, you will be equally enthralled. If you are already familiar with the wonders of grilled cheese, I hope this book will provide fresh inspiration.

GRILLED CHEESE HISTORY

It would seem that the grilled cheese eaters of the 1930s had it right when they dubbed their favorite sandwich the "cheese dream." According to Sylvia Lovegren's *Fashionable Food, Seven Decades of Food Fads* (Macmillan, 1995), Sunday night suppers became popular during that decade, and along with them, the grilled cheese sandwich.

Apparently men in particular were fond of grilled cheese sandwiches, although that may have been for dubious reasons. During this decade, women's clubs became popular, and the food served at the so-called ladies lunches was rather dainty fare such as fruit salad and nutbread sandwiches. But when the "ladies" served this same food to their husbands, it was not so warmly received. The unexpected consequence was the elevation of the simple "cheese dream" to almost gourmet status, for this was one dainty dish the men actually liked. (Of course, *we* might not think of grilled cheese as a "dainty" dish, but times change.)

Although there were many interpretations of the cheese dream, one popular one consisted of two pieces of toasted bread topped with cheese, tomatoes, and ham or bacon. This was broiled and served with pickles and olives. Another, according to Lovegren, was the basic cheese dream, "a plain cheese sandwich cooked in butter in a chafing dish or heavy skillet." She cites *Betty Crocker's Picture Cook Book* (1950) as stating that this version of grilled cheese was invented by boarding school girls as a favorite lunch item, although another version of this sandwich traces back to 1916 and was topped with ketchup.

There are other theories about the origin of the American grilled cheese sandwich. According to the Food Timeline, a compilation of web pages devoted to culinary history, today's grilled cheese sandwich may have made its debut in the 1920s when affordable sliced bread and American cheese came on the market. Recipes from that time were called "toasted cheese" rather than "grilled cheese." (As a term, grilled cheese apparently did not show up until the 1960s.)

But toasted versus grilled reveals a semantics problem that seems to plague the entire subject of grilled cheese. Which cooking method might the recipes have been employing? Sometimes what we call "grilled" is actually toasted. Sometimes it is broiled, as in the English "grilled" cheese sandwich ("grilled" is the English term for broiled). To underscore this confusion, take a look at this recipe for a "Cheese & Ham Toastie" found on a website that culls from English cookery books:

Toasted sandwiches are ordinary sandwiches that have been, well, . . . toasted. Unfortunately, bread is a fairly good insulator, so it needs a slightly more roundabout approach than just sticking a made sandwich under a grill. You need to cook the filling before you cook the outside. Take two matching slices of bread. Cover one edge to edge with thinly sliced or grated cheese and the other with a single slice of shoulder ham. Put them side by side under a roaring grill (or a quiet one if yours is electric) and toast them till the cheese melts and the ham starts to steam and colour. Clap the two halves together and grill the outside, first one side then the other until toasted brown. Then eat.

Notice the word "grill"? In this context, it clearly pertains to the appliance we call a broiler.

England, in fact, was quite likely the place of origin for today's grilled cheese. In the mid-1700s, Elizabeth Raffald gave instructions in her book, *The Experienced English Housewife,* to "toast a light wigg" (a spiced roll) and pour melted cheese over it. In the mid-1800s, another English writer and cook named Eliza Acton had a recipe for "Savoury Toasts." This may very well have been the precursor to America's grilled cheese sandwich because she recommends frying cheese-topped bread in a pan. It is, however, an open-faced sandwich. To finish melting the cheese, she directs the cook to place the sandwich in front of the fire. In that way, it's a two-step process, but it does seem to be a forerunner to the American grilled cheese sandwich.

The French were also influential in America's grilled cheese evolution. The Monte Cristo sandwich, a kind of fried grilled cheese sandwich, is thought to be a successor to the French croque monsieur. Like its French counterpart, the Monte Cristo contains ham and cheese, but it also has turkey or sometimes chicken. The entire sandwich, which is usually made with white or egg bread, is then dipped in egg and pan-fried. It is often sprinkled with powdered sugar and served with jam.

The Monte Cristo sandwich became popular at Disneyland, of all places. Although the Magic Kingdom may seem an unusual venue to launch a culinary staple, its version of the Monte Cristo has been served to countless thousands at the Blue Bayou restaurant in Disneyland's New Orleans Square. While Mickey didn't invent the sandwich, he sure helped put it on the culinary map.

So although the grilled cheese terminology is a bit confusing, in the end the description is less important than the result.

SANDWICH-MAKING TIPS

While almost anyone can put together two slices of bread with a little cheese in the middle, there is an art to making really great grilled cheese sandwiches. After making hundreds of them, I've come up with some tips to help you perfect this simple yet creative sandwich.

THE CHEESE

- *Grate, don't slice.* To melt the cheese sufficiently on the inside of a grilled cheese sandwich without burning the bread, you should grate the cheese rather than slice it. All of the recipes in this book that use firm cheese call for "coarsely grated" cheese. This means using the large holes of a box grater, a rotary grater, or a food processor blade. Some recipes call for two types of cheese, one of which should be finely grated. In that case, use the small holes that are on the smooth side of the grater, not the rough holes that end up making sawdust out of cheese. Alternatively, you can use a rasp grater, such as a Microplane. Use the medium-size rasp rather than the long skinny one, which tends to grate cheese so fine that it resembles delicate snowflakes—you'll end up with a pile of cheese that amounts to mostly air.

- *Pile it on.* In some recipes, the amount of cheese will seem like a lot to fit between two slices of bread. Simply use your palm to compress the cheese after you put it on the bread so that it will fit better. If the cheese doesn't stay inside the bread, read the next tip.
- *Let it ooze.* Don't worry if some cheese comes out of the sandwich onto the pan. Enjoy these toasty little bits in the bottom of the pan—they're the best part!
- *Remove the rind.* Since the rind of a cheese will not melt, always remove it before using the cheese. With soft cheeses like Brie and Camembert it's easiest to do this when the cheese is cold.
- *Grate when cold; cook when warm.* It is easiest to grate cheese when it is cold. However, to ensure perfectly melted cheese, bring the cheese to room temperature before using it.
- *Get a head start.* You can grate the cheese in advance. Simply wrap it tightly in plastic and refrigerate it for up to a day. Bring it to room temperature before using.
- *Grate cheese onto waxed or parchment paper.* Instead of grating cheese onto the counter, try grating it onto waxed or parchment paper. This allows you to easily transport the cheese to another part of the counter while you prepare the rest of the ingredients.

BREAD AND BUTTER

- *Go wild with bread.* Even though the recipes specify particular types of bread, feel free to use whatever you like or happen to have around. For more information, turn to the Bread Lexicon on page 18 for a guide.

- *Size matters.* For the recipes in this book, the bread slices should be the typical sandwich size, or approximately 3 inches by 4 inches, and no more than about ¼-inch thick. Thicker bread will outweigh the filling. If you are using bread from a large, round loaf, you can cut the large center slices in half crosswise.

- *Make a well in a roll.* When used to make grilled cheese, a roll can make the sandwich thick and unwieldy. To avoid this, simply pull out some of the inside of the roll to make a small well or trough. This will create more space for the filling and ensure a crusty sandwich.

- *Compress thick bread and rolls.* All grilled cheese sandwiches should be flattened with a spatula (or perhaps a heavy pan), and this is especially true for thick breads such as focaccia or rolls. Doing this ensures a perfect cheese-to-bread ratio. It also helps the bread cook evenly.

- *Soft is best.* Always use softened butter—it will spread evenly on the bread and make the sandwich brown evenly. If your butter is cold, microwave it for a few seconds at medium power. Just be careful not to leave it in too long or it will melt.

- *Salted butter is best.* Unless otherwise specified, the recipes in this book call for salted butter.

ABOUT COOKING

- *Prepare sandwiches in advance.* One of the many great characteristics of a grilled cheese sandwich is that it can be prepared in advance. You can assemble the sandwiches, wrap them in waxed paper, and refrigerate for up to one day in advance. Unwrap and bring to room temperature before cooking.

- *Size up your skillet.* The type of skillet you use will partially determine how quickly and uniformly your sandwiches will cook. This matters mostly when it comes to melting the cheese. Remember that if the sandwich cooks too fast, the cheese won't melt properly. Unless you have a very large skillet, you may need to cook the sandwiches in batches (or you can use two skillets).

- *Nonstick is best.* Always use a nonstick skillet to make grilled cheese sandwiches. A thin, non-alloy skillet will cook hotter and faster than a thicker, alloy (mixed metal) one. Although a cast-iron skillet is the traditional favorite for grilled cheese, it isn't actually the best pan for it. Cast iron can create a death grip on bread, so when you try to turn the sandwich, much of it will become part of the skillet rather than remain part of the sandwich. This can be avoided if you use copious amounts of butter or oil, but nonstick is easiest and best overall. The same is true for grill pans. They must be greased thoroughly or the sandwich will stick.

- *Adjust the heat #1.* Most of the sandwiches call for medium-high heat. While that will be correct for most stoves, medium-high could lead to charred sandwiches on others. Watch your sandwiches carefully the first time you make them to determine what medium-high means on your stove.

- *Adjust the heat #2.* A few of the recipes call for medium heat when the sandwiches need to cook more slowly—usually the ones that call for breads with high sugar and/or butter content, such as Hawaiian bread, egg bread, and white bread. These breads burn fairly easily and must be cooked a little more slowly. The other sandwiches that should be cooked more slowly are those made with rolls; because it takes longer to cook the bread, it also takes longer to melt the cheese inside. Cooking on lower heat and longer is the key. Be sure to read the directions for each recipe since they're not all the same.

- *Cover it.* Although many recipes for grilled cheese sandwiches do not specify covering the skillet while cooking, I have found that it's best to cover it when cooking the first side of the sandwich in order to melt the cheese sufficiently. Usually it is not necessary to cover the skillet after you've flipped the sandwiches, although a few recipes in the book do call for covering during both phases of cooking, especially when the sandwiches must be cooked at a lower temperature.

ABOUT SANDWICH MAKERS

- *What is a sandwich maker?* If you've traveled to Italy, you've seen the ridged sandwich machines that make the famous sandwiches known as panini. These are made with rolls or sliced bread, and have fillings that consist of anything from just a slice of ham, to cheese, salami, eggplant, or myriad other ingredients. The lid of the panini maker is gently lowered onto the sandwich, and after about 3 minutes, out comes a sandwich with grill-like marks and a warmed-through filling.

  In this country, the most popular equivalent of an Italian panini maker is the George Foreman grill. It too is a ridged machine that compresses and grills a sandwich on both sides simultaneously (with much wider grill marks). There are many other brands of sandwich makers (sometimes called panini makers in this country as well), each of them sporting different features such as variable temperature settings and adjustable lids to accommodate different-sized sandwiches. If your sandwich maker has temperature settings, for most recipes you should set it to medium-high, though some specify medium heat.

One of the best things about these machines is that they cook grilled cheese sandwiches and quesadillas very quickly. They also ensure crispy bread or tortillas every time.

- *Use butter or oil sparingly.* Most sandwich makers are made with nonstick surfaces. As a result, it isn't necessary to butter or brush oil on your bread before cooking the sandwiches. However, if you like the added flavor that comes from butter or oil, then by all means use it. All the recipes here call for either butter or oil. You might try using a little less—not only does the sandwich maker allow for this; it also encourages it because of its nonstick surface. That is, much of the butter or oil can end up on the cooking surface rather than in the sandwich. The best way to know how much to use is to experiment with your machine.

- *Waffle irons really work!* If you don't have a sandwich maker, but you do have an old (or new) waffle iron sitting around, now is the time to use it. Grilled cheese sandwiches work just fine in these. Of course, the sandwich will look more like a waffle, but that's part of the fun.

USING THE GRILL

- *Gas is better than charcoal or wood.* Although you can technically barbecue sandwiches, it probably isn't the best way to showcase a grilled cheese because it inevitably ends up tasting more like the wood or charcoal than the cheese or bread. For this reason, I recommend using a gas grill only, because it will bring out, rather than mask, the flavors of the sandwich, and you can regulate the heat better.

BREAD LEXICON

The type of bread used to make a grilled cheese sandwich can make all the difference. If you've got a heavy filling, then you need to have a hearty bread. If you're making a sweet grilled cheese sandwich, then use a lighter-style bread—an egg or white bread is best. Although white, rye, wheat, and sourdough breads are readily available, not everyone can get every type of bread where they live. For that reason, I have compiled the following list to help you understand the more unusual types of breads as well as their closest substitutes. After making a few sandwiches, you will probably discover your favorite breads for grilled cheese. By all means, use them!

All sandwiches in this book call for ¼-inch-thick slices of bread, except for those that specify rolls or focaccia. Regular sandwich bread is the right size and thickness. Use those slices as your guide if you choose to buy whole loaves of bread and slice them yourself.

CIABATTA Also known as Italian "slipper" bread, ciabatta is so named because of its flat, shoe-like shape. It has a light-colored, brittle crust that is lightly dusted with flour. The interior of this bread is rather airy yet also somewhat doughy, owing to the unusually large amount of water used to make it.

Substitute: Pugliese (sometimes called *pane pugliese*) or light sourdough.

FOCACCIA This is an Italian flat bread made with olive oil, and is somewhat doughy in the middle and slightly crispy on the bottom and sometimes the top. Focaccia can be simple, adorned with just olive oil and a little sea salt, or it can be more elaborate and made with a variety of different ingredients including herbs, garlic, tomatoes, olives, cheese, or sometimes fruit (such as grapes). It is a yeast dough—similar to pizza dough—that is made in a rectangular shape, and is typically about ¾ inch thick.

Substitute: Because most other breads are crustier than focaccia, there isn't a perfect substitute. Look for a not-too-crusty flat bread—many bread bakeries make their own version of flat bread. Or, if you can't find that, then you can take a large loaf of a hearty Italian or French bread, cut off the crusts, and cut the bread into ¾-inch-thick slices.

HAWAIIAN BREAD Sometimes called Hawaiian sweet bread and also Portuguese sweet bread, Hawaiian bread is a soft, sweet bread made with eggs, sugar, butter, flour, and sometimes other ingredients such as pineapple juice. It is very soft and delicate in texture.

Substitute: Egg bread or brioche. These breads are not sweet like Hawaiian bread, but they are similar otherwise. Depending on the recipe, you can add sugar to the filling to approximate the flavor of Hawaiian bread.

OLIVE BREAD This may contain black or green olives—or both—and the bread is usually made with olive oil and some amount of whole wheat flour. Occasionally, herbs are added as well.

Substitute: There is no direct substitute for olive bread, so use a hearty Italian bread or *pain au levain* (see page 20) and add pitted and chopped Italian, French, or Spanish olives to the sandwich.

PAIN AU LEVAIN This is a bread made with a sourdough starter. It is, in fact, the French word for sourdough. It is a tangy, chewy, slightly more dense bread than conventional sourdough.

Substitute: Sourdough, whole wheat sourdough, or hearty Italian bread.

ABOUT CHEESE

Although most of the cheeses called for in this book are well known, there are a few that may be less familiar. Rather than including a list of every cheese available (there are thousands!), what follows is a guide to the different styles of cheese and the best-known cheeses within those categories. Use this to help figure out substitute cheeses if necessary. Or simply use it to help understand cheese a little better.

FRESH CHEESE This is cheese that is unripened—that is, not aged. Examples are fromage blanc, cottage cheese, fresh goat cheese, ricotta, and mozzarella. (Mozzarella is in this category because it is an unaged cheese. Because of its texture, it also fits into the semi-soft category.)

SEMI-SOFT CHEESE This is creamy to moderately firm cheese. Examples include Monterey Jack, California Teleme, Crescenza, Colby, some Goudas, young cheddars, and Havarti.

SOFT-RIPENED CHEESE The familiar cheese that has a white rind (also called a "bloomy" rind) that is the result of a beneficial mold that is added to the milk and/or sprayed on the cheese during aging. It is called "soft-ripened" cheese because it gets softer rather than harder as it ripens or ages. Bloomy rind cheese is also distinctive because it ripens from the outside toward the center. That is why there is often a translucent, creamy layer just underneath the rind. Examples are Brie and Camembert.

SEMI-HARD CHEESE Rather firm cheese that bends but doesn't crumble. It usually has a creamy or smooth feeling in the mouth. Examples are Swiss, Gruyère, Emmentaler, Appenzeller, cheddar, and some Goudas.

HARD CHEESE This type of cheese is the result of a long aging period. The longer a cheese is exposed to air, the more moisture it will lose, and this creates the harder texture. Examples are any super-aged cheese such as Parmigiano-Reggiano, aged Gouda, and dry Monterey Jack.

WASHED-RIND CHEESE This is the most aromatic group, but usually the aroma is stronger than the taste. The texture of washed-rind cheese ranges from creamy to semi-soft, while its flavor ranges from mild to "stinky." Examples are Red Hawk (Cowgirl Creamery), Epoisses, Munster (Alsatian—not American), Taleggio, Pont l'Évêque, and Reblochon.

BLUE CHEESE Distinguished by the *Penicillium roqueforti* or the *penicillium glaucom* mold, blue cheese varies widely in texture, flavor, and style. Gorgonzola is often softer and sometimes sweet, as in Gorgonzola dolce (an exception is mountain Gorgonzola, which is aged quite a long time and becomes fairly hard). Other blue cheese is creamy and crumbly with a tangy flavor. This would include Maytag Blue, Pt. Reyes Farmstead Cheese Company's Original Blue, and Great Hill Blue from Massachusetts. Other creamy-style blue cheeses are Saga blue and Cambozola. Yet another style of blue is hard and crumbly. Examples are classic Stilton and Rustic Blue from Bingham Hill Cheese Company in Colorado.

CLASSIC GRILLED CHEESE

Original American Grilled Cheese

The Best Grilled Cheese

Classic (and Easy) Reuben

French-Style Grilled Ham and Cheese

Dutch Grilled Cheese

ORIGINAL AMERICAN GRILLED CHEESE

*S*ome may argue that a grilled cheese sandwich with American cheese slices needs no recipe, but here it is. If you'd like to update it slightly, then use potato bread or country-style white bread, which is a little heartier and will hold up a bit better when grilled.

> 8 slices white sandwich bread (¼ inch thick)
> 2 tablespoons butter, at room temperature
> 8 slices American cheese

To assemble: Butter one side of each slice of bread. Place 4 slices on your work surface, buttered side down. Distribute the cheese evenly over the 4 slices. Place the remaining 4 bread slices on top, buttered side up.

STOVETOP METHOD Heat a large nonstick skillet over medium-high heat for 2 minutes. Put the sandwiches in the skillet (in batches if necessary), cover, and cook for 2 minutes, or until the undersides are golden brown and the cheese has begun to melt. Uncover, and turn the sandwiches with a spatula, pressing firmly to flatten them slightly. Cook for 1 minute, or until the undersides are golden brown. Turn the sandwiches again, press with the spatula, and cook for 30 seconds, or until the cheese has melted completely. Serve immediately.

SANDWICH MAKER METHOD Preheat the sandwich maker. Follow directions for sandwich assembly, and cook according to the manufacturer's instructions.

GAS GRILL METHOD Brush the grill rack with oil and preheat the grill to medium-high. Follow directions for sandwich assembly. Put the sandwiches on the grill and follow directions for the stovetop method.

MAKES 4 SANDWICHES

THE BEST GRILLED CHEESE

*A*lthough most people seem to have their own version of the "best" grilled cheese sandwich, this one defines grilled cheese as it was meant to be: crunchy bread and perfectly melted cheese.

>   8 slices sourdough bread (¼ inch thick)
>   2 tablespoons butter, at room temperature
>   6 ounces best-quality cheddar cheese (orange or white),
>   coarsely grated

To assemble: Butter one side of each slice of bread. Place 4 slices on your work surface, buttered side down. Distribute the cheese evenly over the 4 slices. Place the remaining 4 bread slices on top, buttered side up.

STOVETOP METHOD Heat a large nonstick skillet over medium-high heat for 2 minutes. Put the sandwiches in the skillet (in batches if necessary), cover, and cook for 2 minutes, or until the undersides are golden brown and the cheese has begun to melt. Uncover, and turn the sandwiches with a spatula, pressing firmly to flatten them slightly. Cook for 1 minute, or until the undersides are golden brown. Turn the sandwiches again, press with the spatula, and cook for 30 seconds, or until the cheese has melted completely. Serve immediately.

SANDWICH MAKER METHOD Preheat the sandwich maker. Follow directions for sandwich assembly, and cook according to the manufacturer's instructions.

GAS GRILL METHOD Brush the grill rack with oil and preheat the grill to medium-high. Follow directions for sandwich assembly. Put the sandwiches on the grill and follow directions for the stovetop method.

MAKES 4 SANDWICHES

CLASSIC (AND EASY) REUBEN

*A*lthough *many people think of corned beef as the star of a Reuben sandwich, to me, it is the melted cheese that gets top billing. This classic sandwich is full-flavored and a wonderful treat that need not be confined to the deli experience.*

FOR THE DRESSING
¼ cup mayonnaise
¼ cup chili sauce
1 teaspoon pickle relish

4 ounces Emmentaler cheese, coarsely grated
4 ounces Gruyère cheese, coarsely grated
2 tablespoons butter, at room temperature
8 slices rye bread (¼ inch thick)
½ pound cooked corned beef, thinly sliced
1 can (14.5 ounces) sauerkraut, drained

To make the dressing: In a small bowl, mix together the mayonnaise, chili sauce, and relish. Set aside. (The dressing can be made up to 1 day in advance and refrigerated.)

In a small bowl, mix the cheeses together. Set aside.

To assemble: Butter one side of each slice of bread. Place 4 slices on your work surface, buttered side down. Spread about 2 tablespoons of the dressing on each of the 4 slices. Distribute the corned beef evenly over the dressing, followed by the sauerkraut and cheese. (You may need to press down on the cheese to make it fit. Don't worry if you leave a few shavings behind.) Place the remaining 4 bread slices on top, buttered side up.

STOVETOP METHOD Heat a large nonstick skillet over medium-high heat for 2 minutes. Put the sandwiches in the skillet (in batches if necessary), cover, and cook for 2 to 3 minutes, or until the undersides are golden brown and the cheese has begun to melt. Uncover, and turn the sandwiches with a spatula, pressing firmly to flatten them slightly. Cook for 1 to 2 minutes more, or until the undersides are golden brown. Turn the sandwiches again, press with the spatula, and cook for 30 seconds, or until the cheese has melted completely. Serve immediately.

SANDWICH MAKER METHOD Preheat the sandwich maker. Follow directions for sandwich assembly, and cook according to the manufacturer's instructions.

GAS GRILL METHOD Brush the grill rack with oil and preheat the grill to medium-high. Follow directions for sandwich assembly. Put the sandwiches on the grill and follow directions for the stovetop method.

MAKES 4 SANDWICHES

FRENCH-STYLE GRILLED HAM AND CHEESE

he traditional cheese sandwich of France is the croque monsieur. Consisting of Gruyère cheese and thin-sliced ham, it is usually cooked under a broiler or in a special pan. Although this recipe calls for the traditional cheese and ham, I've embellished it by adding another classic French combination: tarragon and Dijon mustard. Together, these ingredients make for an herbaceous, tangy, and memorable grilled cheese sandwich.

6 ounces Gruyère cheese, coarsely grated
2 teaspoons chopped fresh tarragon (or ¾ teaspoon dried)
2 tablespoons butter, at room temperature
8 slices egg bread (¼ inch thick)
¼ pound Black Forest ham, cut into 4 slices
2 tablespoons Dijon mustard, plus extra for serving

In a small bowl, mix together the cheese and tarragon. Set aside.

To assemble: Butter one side of each slice of bread. Place 4 slices on your work surface, buttered side down. Distribute the cheese mixture evenly over the 4 slices. Cover the cheese with the ham, folding it to fit if necessary. Spread the mustard on the remaining 4 bread slices and place them on top of the ham, mustard side down.

STOVETOP METHOD Heat a large nonstick skillet over medium-high heat for 2 minutes. Put the sandwiches in the skillet (in batches if necessary), cover, and cook for 2 minutes, or until the undersides are golden brown and the cheese has begun to melt. Uncover, and turn the sandwiches with a spatula, pressing firmly to flatten them slightly. Cook for 1 minute, or until the undersides are golden brown. Turn the sandwiches again, press with the spatula, and cook for 30 seconds, or until the cheese has melted completely. Serve immediately, with extra mustard on the side.

SANDWICH MAKER METHOD Preheat the sandwich maker. Follow directions for sandwich assembly, and cook according to the manufacturer's instructions.

GAS GRILL METHOD Brush the grill rack with oil and preheat the grill to medium-high. Follow directions for sandwich assembly. Put the sandwiches on the grill and follow directions for the stovetop method.

MAKES 4 SANDWICHES

DUTCH GRILLED CHEESE

G ouda cheese, cumin, and caraway combine to produce a distinctive and flavorful sandwich with a taste that is reminiscent of the traditional Dutch Leyden cheese.

3 tablespoons butter, at room temperature
1 medium red onion (about ½ pound), thinly sliced
¾ teaspoon cumin seeds
6 ounces best-quality medium-aged Gouda cheese, coarsely grated
8 slices rye bread with caraway seeds (¼ inch thick)

In a large nonstick skillet, melt 1 tablespoon of the butter over low heat. Add the onions and cook very slowly, stirring occasionally, until they turn a dark golden color, 30 to 40 minutes. If the onions begin to scorch, add about 1 tablespoon of water. Remove the onions from pan and set aside. Wipe the skillet with a paper towel, but do not wash it. (The onions can be prepared up to 6 hours in advance and kept covered at room temperature.)

Heat the same skillet over medium-high heat. Add the cumin seeds and toast just until they become fragrant, about 3 minutes (watch carefully, they burn easily). Remove the seeds and let cool briefly. Do not wash the skillet. When the seeds are cool, crush them using a mortar and pestle. Or place them in a resealable plastic bag and lightly pound with a mallet or the bottom of a heavy skillet. In a medium bowl, toss the crushed seeds with the cheese.

To assemble: Butter one side of each slice of bread with the remaining 2 tablespoons butter. Place 4 slices on your work surface, buttered

side down. Distribute the cheese evenly over the 4 slices, followed by the onions. Place the remaining 4 bread slices on top, buttered side up.

STOVETOP METHOD Heat the same skillet over medium-high heat for 2 minutes. Put the sandwiches in the skillet (in batches if necessary), cover, and cook for 2 minutes, or until the undersides are golden brown and the cheese has begun to melt. Uncover, and turn the sandwiches with a spatula, pressing firmly to flatten them slightly. Cook for 1 minute, or until the undersides are golden brown. Turn the sandwiches again, press with the spatula, and cook for 30 seconds, or until the cheese has melted completely. Serve immediately.

SANDWICH MAKER METHOD Preheat the sandwich maker. Follow directions for sandwich assembly, and cook according to the manufacturer's instructions.

GAS GRILL METHOD Brush the grill rack with oil and preheat the grill to medium-high. Follow directions for sandwich assembly. Put the sandwiches on the grill and follow directions for the stovetop method.

MAKES 4 SANDWICHES

ALMOST-CLASSIC GRILLED CHEESE

Havarti and Dilled Cucumbers on Rye

Apple, Ham, and Cheddar on Sourdough

Spicy Double-Jack

Salami and Cheese #1

Salami and Cheese #2

Buffalo Chicken Sandwich

Four-Cheese Italian on Ciabatta

Roast Beef with Cheddar and Blue Cheese Butter

Cheesy Gashouse Egg Sandwich

Feta and Eggplant on Pita with Sesame-Yogurt Sauce

Crab-Feta Melt

Grilled Caprese

HAVARTI AND DILLED CUCUMBERS ON RYE

One of America's favorite cheeses is dill-flavored Havarti. For this delectable sandwich, I decided to bring Havarti and dill together in a different way—I flavor the sweet-and-sour cucumbers with dill and then top them with the creamy cheese.

FOR THE CUCUMBERS

¼ cup cider vinegar

¼ cup water

2 tablespoons sugar

1 teaspoon salt

½ teaspoon dried dill (or 2 teaspoons chopped fresh dill)

2 medium cucumbers, peeled and cut into ⅛- to ¼-inch-thick slices

6 ounces Havarti cheese, coarsely grated

2 tablespoons butter, at room temperature

8 slices rye bread (¼ inch thick)

To prepare the cucumbers: In a medium bowl, stir together the vinegar, water, sugar, salt, and dill. Add the cucumbers and stir to coat. Let sit for at least 15 minutes and for up to 2 hours. (The cucumbers can be prepared up to 1 day in advance and refrigerated. Bring to room temperature before using.)

To assemble: Butter one side of each slice of bread. Place 4 slices on your work surface, buttered side down. Using a slotted spoon, drain the cucumbers slightly and distribute them evenly over the 4 slices, followed by the cheese. Place the remaining 4 bread slices on top, buttered side up.

STOVETOP METHOD Heat a large nonstick skillet over medium-high heat for 2 minutes. Put the sandwiches in the skillet (in batches if necessary), cover, and cook for 2 minutes, or until the undersides are golden brown and the cheese has begun to melt. Uncover, and turn the sandwiches with a spatula, pressing firmly to flatten them slightly. Cook for 1 to 2 minutes more, or until the undersides are golden brown. Turn the sandwiches again, press with the spatula, and cook for 30 seconds to 1 minute, or until the cheese has melted completely. Serve immediately.

SANDWICH MAKER METHOD Preheat the sandwich maker. Follow directions for sandwich assembly, and cook according to the manufacturer's instructions.

GAS GRILL METHOD Brush the grill rack with oil and preheat the grill to medium-high. Follow directions for sandwich assembly. Put the sandwiches on the grill and follow directions for the stovetop method.

MAKES 4 SANDWICHES

APPLE, HAM, AND CHEDDAR ON SOURDOUGH

Cheddar and apple is a classic combination as is cheddar and ham. So why not combine America's favorite cheese with apples and ham and grill them? Best of all, you need no special ingredients to make this homey taste sensation.

> 2 tablespoons butter, at room temperature
> 8 slices sourdough bread (¼ inch thick)
> ¼ pound smoky ham, such as Virginia country ham, cut into
>   4 slices (or buy pre-sliced ham)
> 1 small green apple (about 5 ounces), such as Granny Smith,
>   cut into ⅛-inch-thick slices
> 6 ounces medium or sharp cheddar cheese, coarsely grated

To assemble: Butter one side of each slice of bread. Place 4 slices on your work surface, buttered side down. Place a slice of ham on each bread slice, folding it to fit if necessary. Top with 4 to 5 apple slices per sandwich, followed by the cheese. Place the remaining 4 bread slices on top, buttered side up. (If the sandwich seems quite thick, press it down to compress the ingredients slightly.)

STOVETOP METHOD Heat a large nonstick skillet over medium-high heat for 2 minutes. Put the sandwiches in the skillet (in batches if necessary), cover, and cook for 2 minutes, or until the undersides are golden brown and the cheese has begun to melt. Uncover, and turn the sandwiches with a spatula, pressing firmly to flatten them slightly. Cook for 1 minute, or until the undersides are golden brown. Turn the sandwiches again, press with the spatula, and cook for 30 seconds, or until the cheese has melted completely. Serve immediately.

SANDWICH MAKER METHOD Preheat the sandwich maker. Follow directions for sandwich assembly, and cook according to the manufacturer's instructions.

GAS GRILL METHOD Brush the grill rack with oil and preheat the grill to medium-high. Follow directions for sandwich assembly. Put the sandwiches on the grill and follow directions for the stovetop method.

MAKES 4 SANDWICHES

SPICY DOUBLE-JACK

Most of us think of the American grilled cheese as having some type of cheddar or processed American cheese, but Monterey Jack is truly an American original, having been invented in California in the 1800s. The addition of spicy pepper flakes to this sandwich gives it an appropriate California touch, and the use of dry Jack cheese further extends the all-American theme. Keep a close eye on these during cooking, as the cheese-butter on the outside can burn easily.

1 ounce dry Jack cheese (or use Parmesan), finely grated

6 ounces Monterey Jack cheese, coarsely grated

2 teaspoons red pepper flakes (or use 1½ teaspoons for a less spicy sandwich)

2 tablespoons butter, at room temperature

8 slices sourdough or Italian country bread (¼ inch thick)

In a small bowl, stir together the butter and dry Jack until it becomes pastelike. In another small bowl, toss together the Monterey Jack and pepper flakes. Set aside.

To assemble: Butter one side of each slice of bread with the cheese-butter. Place 4 slices on your work surface, buttered side down. Distribute the cheese–pepper flake mixture evenly over the 4 slices. Place the remaining 4 bread slices on top, buttered side up.

STOVETOP METHOD Heat a large nonstick skillet over medium-high heat for 2 minutes. Put the sandwiches in the skillet (in batches if necessary), cover, and cook for 2 minutes, or until the undersides are golden brown and the cheese has begun to melt. Uncover, and turn the sandwiches with a spatula, pressing firmly to flatten them slightly.

Cook for 1 minute, or until the undersides are golden brown. Turn the sandwiches again, press with the spatula, and cook for 30 seconds, or until the cheese has melted completely. Serve immediately.

SANDWICH MAKER METHOD Preheat the sandwich maker. Follow directions for sandwich assembly, and cook according to the manufacturer's instructions. Watch the sandwiches carefully as the cheese-butter mixture on the outside of the bread can burn easily.

GAS GRILL METHOD Brush the grill rack with oil and preheat the grill to medium-high. Follow directions for sandwich assembly. Put the sandwiches on the grill and follow directions for the stovetop method.

MAKES 4 SANDWICHES

SALAMI AND CHEESE #1

*T*he combination of cheeses, salami, and peppers in this sandwich makes it very similar to the ever-popular hero sandwich. The big difference is that this one is cooked.

> 1 tablespoon fennel seed
> ¼ cup olive oil
> 12 paper-thin slices of 2-inch-diameter salami (about 1 ounce)
> 8 slices Italian bread (¼ inch thick) or use four 3-inch-wide pieces of ciabatta (cut in half; pull out some of the center of each piece to create a well)
> 4 ounces ricotta cheese, at room temperature (drain if watery)
> Freshly ground pepper
> 6 ounces mozzarella cheese, coarsely grated
> 12 pepperoncini, stemmed, halved lengthwise, seeded, and drained

In a small skillet, heat the fennel seeds over medium-high heat. Shake the pan occasionally and cook until the seeds darken and begin to emit a toasty aroma, 2 to 3 minutes. One or two seeds may pop. Let cool slightly. Using a mortar and pestle or a spice grinder, crush the seeds until they're very fine, almost powder-like. (Alternatively, you can place the seeds in a resealable plastic bag and lightly pound them with a mallet or the bottom of a heavy skillet.)

In a small bowl, stir together the oil and crushed fennel seed. Set aside.

Heat a large nonstick skillet over medium heat for 2 minutes. Add the salami and cook until it begins to brown, 2 to 3 minutes. Turn and cook for about 3 minutes, or until the slices have begun to shrink and turn golden brown. Transfer the salami to a plate. Wipe the skillet with a paper towel, but do not wash it.

To assemble: Brush one side of each slice of bread with the reserved fennel oil. Place 4 slices on your work surface, oiled side down. Spread the ricotta on the 4 slices and add pepper to taste. Distribute the mozzarella evenly over the 4 slices, followed by the pepperoncini and the salami. Place the remaining 4 bread slices on top, oiled side up.

STOVETOP METHOD Heat the large skillet over medium-high heat for 2 minutes. Put the sandwiches in the skillet (in batches if necessary), cover, and cook for 2 minutes, or until the undersides are golden brown and the cheese has begun to melt. Uncover, and turn the sandwiches with a spatula, pressing firmly to flatten them slightly. Cook for 1 minute, or until the undersides are golden brown. Turn the sandwiches again, press with the spatula, and cook for 30 seconds, or until the mozzarella has melted completely. Serve immediately.

SANDWICH MAKER METHOD Preheat the sandwich maker. Follow directions for sandwich assembly, and cook according to the manufacturer's instructions.

GAS GRILL METHOD Brush the grill rack with oil and preheat the grill to medium-high. Follow directions for sandwich assembly. Put the sandwiches on the grill and follow directions for the stovetop method.

MAKES 4 SANDWICHES

SALAMI AND CHEESE #2

I t's worth going the extra mile to seek out the olive bread for this
recipe, but if you can't find it, add ¼ cup chopped olives to the
sandwich filling. It isn't quite the same, but it's a fine substitute.

> 12 paper-thin slices of 2-inch-diameter salami (about 1
> ounce)
> 2 tablespoons olive oil
> 8 slices olive bread, ¼ inch thick (or use a hearty Italian or
> wheat bread)
> 6 ounces Italian Fontina cheese, coarsely grated

Preheat a large nonstick skillet over medium heat for 2 minutes.
Add the salami and cook until it begins to brown, 2 to 3 minutes. Turn
and cook for about 3 minutes, or until the slices have begun to shrink
and turn golden brown. Transfer the salami to a plate. Wipe the skillet
with a paper towel, but do not wash it.

To assemble: Brush one side of each slice of bread with the oil.
Place 4 slices on your work surface, oiled side down. Distribute the
cheese evenly over the 4 slices, followed by the salami. Place the
remaining 4 bread slices on top, oiled side up.

STOVETOP METHOD Heat the same skillet over medium-high heat for 2
minutes. Put the sandwiches in the skillet (in batches if necessary),
cover, and cook for 2 minutes, or until the undersides are golden
brown and the cheese has begun to melt. Uncover, and turn the sandwiches with a spatula, pressing firmly to flatten them slightly. Cook
for 1 minute, or until the undersides are golden brown. Turn the

sandwiches again, press with the spatula, and cook for 30 seconds, or until the cheese has melted completely. Serve immediately.

SANDWICH MAKER METHOD Preheat the sandwich maker. Follow directions for sandwich assembly, and cook according to the manufacturer's instructions.

GAS GRILL METHOD Brush the grill rack with oil and preheat the grill to medium-high. Follow directions for sandwich assembly. Put the sandwiches on the grill and follow directions for the stovetop method.

MAKES 4 SANDWICHES

BUFFALO CHICKEN SANDWICH

If you've ever been to Buffalo, New York, or anywhere in the country that offers its version of "Buffalo wings," you'll know what this sandwich holds in store. It's spicy, salty, and crunchy, too. But it parts ways with the original, since chicken wings don't fly in a sandwich. Buffalo wings are traditionally served with celery and blue cheese dressing on the side, but I've put all the ingredients right in the sandwich. To simplify, you can use your favorite blue cheese dressing instead of making the spread.

FOR THE SPREAD

5 ounces creamy blue cheese, crumbled

¼ cup mayonnaise

¼ cup sour cream

2 teaspoons lemon juice

2 tablespoons chopped chives

1 rib celery, finely chopped, plus extra ribs for serving

Freshly ground pepper

FOR THE SAUCE

4 tablespoons (½ stick) butter

1½ tablespoons hot sauce

1½ teaspoons cider vinegar

FOR THE CHICKEN

¼ cup olive oil

2 whole skinless boneless chicken breasts (about 2 pounds),
   cut in half lengthwise and pounded ¼ inch thick

Salt and freshly ground pepper

Four 4-inch pieces of focaccia, cut in half (or use soft rolls or
   sourdough)

To make the spread: In a medium bowl stir all the spread ingredients together until well blended. Set aside. (The spread can be made up to 2 days in advance and refrigerated.)

To make the sauce: In a small saucepan, combine the sauce ingredients and cook over low heat until the butter is melted. Keep warm over the lowest setting on your stove.

STOVETOP METHOD *To prepare the chicken:* Heat 2 tablespoons of the oil in a large nonstick skillet over medium-high heat. Place the chicken in the skillet and cook for 2 minutes or until the undersides are no longer pink. Turn and cook 2 to 3 minutes more, or until the chicken has turned a light brown color and feels firm to the touch but still slightly springy. Remove from the heat and set aside just until the chicken is cool enough to handle.

Dip the chicken pieces into the sauce, making sure they are thoroughly coated, then set them on a plate. Wipe the skillet with a paper towel, but do not wash it.

To assemble: Pull out some of the center of each piece of bread to make a well. Brush the outside of each piece with the remaining 2 tablespoons oil. Place the 4 bottom pieces on your work surface, oiled side down. Spread about 2 tablespoons of the spread on each and top with a piece of chicken. Place the remaining 4 pieces of bread, on top, oiled side up.

To cook: Heat the same skillet over medium-high heat for 2 minutes. Put the sandwiches into the skillet, press firmly with a spatula to compress the bread, cover, and cook for 2 to 3 minutes or until the undersides are golden brown. Uncover, and turn the sandwiches, press with the spatula, and cook for 1 to 2 minutes, or until the undersides are a deep golden brown. Turn again and cook for 30 seconds. Serve with extra blue cheese spread and celery on the side.

SANDWICH MAKER METHOD Preheat the sandwich maker.

To prepare the chicken: Place the chicken in the sandwich maker and close the lid. Cook just until the chicken has turned a shade or two darker and feels firm to the touch but still slightly springy, 3 to 4 minutes (if you have a ridged sandwich maker, the chicken will have pronounced grill marks). Remove the chicken and set aside just until it is cool enough to handle.

Dip the chicken pieces into the sauce, making sure they are thoroughly coated, then set them on a plate.

To assemble: Follow directions for sandwich assembly for the stovetop method.

To cook: Place the sandwiches in the sandwich maker and cook until they have compressed by about one-third, 3 to 4 minutes. Serve with extra blue cheese spread and celery on the side.

GAS GRILL METHOD Brush the grill rack with oil and preheat the grill to medium-high.

To prepare the chicken: Place the chicken on the grill, cover, and cook 3 to 4 minutes, or until light grill marks have formed. Turn and cook 2 to 3 minutes more, or until the chicken feels firm to the touch but still slightly springy. Remove from the grill and set aside just until it is cool enough to handle.

Dip the chicken pieces into the sauce, making sure they are thoroughly coated, then set them on a plate.

To assemble and cook: Follow assembly directions for the stovetop method. Put the sandwiches on the grill and follow cooking directions for the stovetop method.

MAKES 4 SANDWICHES

FOUR-CHEESE ITALIAN ON CIABATTA

*B*ecause *this sandwich calls for thick bread, it is best to pinch out
some of the center to make room for the filling. This leaves mostly
crust behind, making the sandwich almost like a cheesy, gooey pizza.*

> 2 ounces ricotta cheese, at room temperature (drain if watery)
> 2 ounces Parmesan cheese, finely grated
> Freshly ground pepper
> 1 loaf ciabatta, cut into four 3-inch-wide sections and halved
>   (or use 4 ciabatta rolls or 8 slices hearty Italian or
>   sourdough bread)
> 2 tablespoons olive oil
> 4 ounces Fontina cheese, coarsely grated
> 4 ounces mozzarella cheese, coarsely grated (if cheese is
>   watery, drain and cut in small chunks, rather than grate)

In a small bowl, mix together the ricotta and Parmesan cheeses, and
add pepper to taste. Set aside.

To assemble: Pull out some of the center of each piece of bread to
create a well, and brush each piece with the oil. Place 4 pieces on your
work surface, oiled side down. Spread the reserved cheese mixture
evenly over the 4 pieces. Distribute the Fontina and mozzarella evenly
over the top. Place the remaining 4 bread slices on top, oiled side up.

STOVETOP METHOD Heat a large nonstick skillet over medium heat for
2 minutes. Put the sandwiches in the skillet (in batches if necessary),
cover, and cook for 2 to 3 minutes, or until the undersides are golden
brown and the cheese has begun to melt. Uncover, and turn the sandwiches with a spatula, pressing firmly to flatten them slightly. Cook for

1 to 2 minutes, or until the undersides are golden brown. Turn the sandwiches again, press with the spatula, and cook for 30 seconds, or until the cheese has melted completely. Serve immediately.

SANDWICH MAKER METHOD Preheat the sandwich maker. If your machine has adjustable heat, set it to medium. Follow directions for sandwich assembly, and cook until the rolls are a shade darker and the cheese has melted completely.

GAS GRILL METHOD Brush the grill rack with oil and preheat the grill to medium. Follow directions for sandwich assembly. Put the sandwiches on the grill and follow directions for the stovetop method.

MAKES 4 SANDWICHES

ROAST BEEF WITH CHEDDAR AND BLUE CHEESE BUTTER

Roast beef and cheddar is a classic pairing, but when grilled with blue cheese butter and topped with onion jam, it soars into "extraordinary" territory. I hope you'll agree.

FOR THE JAM
2 tablespoons salted butter
1 medium onion (about ½ pound), thinly sliced
¼ teaspoon salt
1 tablespoon packed light brown sugar

2 ounces blue cheese
2 tablespoons unsalted butter
8 slices sourdough bread (¼ inch thick)
¼ pound cooked roast beef, thinly sliced
6 ounces sharp cheddar cheese, coarsely grated

To make the jam: In a large nonstick skillet, melt the salted butter over medium-high heat. Add the onions and cook, stirring occasionally, until they are lightly golden, about 6 minutes. Reduce heat to low and cook, stirring occasionally, until the onions are a deep golden color, 8 to 10 minutes. Add the salt and brown sugar, and stir until the sugar has dissolved and the onions look glazed, about 1 minute. Remove the onions from the pan and let cool. (The jam can be prepared up to 6 hours in advance and kept covered at room temperature.)

In a small bowl, mash the blue cheese and unsalted butter together.

To assemble: Spread the blue cheese butter on one side of each slice of bread. Place 4 slices on your work surface, buttered side down.

Distribute the roast beef evenly over the 4 slices, followed by the cheddar cheese. Spoon on the jam, and top with the remaining 4 bread slices, buttered side up.

STOVETOP METHOD Heat a large nonstick skillet over medium-high heat for 2 minutes. Put the sandwiches in the skillet (in batches if necessary), cover, and cook for 2 minutes, or until the undersides are golden brown and the cheese has begun to melt. Uncover, and turn the sandwiches with a spatula, pressing firmly to flatten them slightly. Cook for 1 minute, or until the undersides are golden brown. Turn the sandwiches again, press with the spatula, and cook for 30 seconds, or until the cheese has melted completely. Serve immediately.

SANDWICH MAKER METHOD Preheat the sandwich maker. Follow directions for sandwich assembly, and cook according to the manufacturer's instructions. Watch the sandwiches carefully as the blue cheese butter can burn easily.

GAS GRILL METHOD Brush the grill rack with oil and preheat the grill to medium-high. Follow directions for sandwich assembly. Put the sandwiches on the grill and follow directions for the stovetop method.

MAKES 4 SANDWICHES

CHEESY GASHOUSE EGG SANDWICH

When we were kids, my friend Dana and I had a favorite breakfast we called "gashouse" eggs. You made a hole in the center of a piece of bread, placed it in a skillet, dropped an egg into the hole, and fried it—think fried egg and toast all in one. Although a gashouse egg doesn't usually call for cheese, I was inspired to come up with this homey grilled cheese-and-egg sandwich.

2 tablespoons butter, at room temperature

8 slices white, wheat, or egg bread (¼ inch thick)

6 ounces Monterey Jack, Swiss, or Gruyère cheese, coarsely grated

4 large eggs

Salt and freshly ground pepper

Have a small bowl or cup ready.

To assemble: Butter one side of each slice of bread, and place on your work surface, buttered side down. Using a 2¼-inch-diameter glass (such as a juice glass) or a sharp knife, cut a 2¼-inch hole in the center of each bread slice. Press the cheese evenly onto 4 bread slices around the hole. (It may seem like a lot of cheese, but you'll see that it's the perfect amount. It's okay if a few bits of cheese are left behind.) Place the remaining 4 bread slices on top, buttered side up.

[STOVETOP METHOD] Heat a large nonstick skillet over a medium-*low* heat for 2 minutes. Put the sandwiches in the skillet (in batches if necessary), cover, and cook for 2 to 3 minutes, or until the undersides turn golden brown. Turn the sandwiches and, working quickly, separate 1 egg over the small cup, allowing the egg white to drip into the cup.

Pour the yolk into the hole in the bread and then pour the egg white over it. Sprinkle with salt and pepper to taste. Repeat with remaining eggs and sandwiches.

Cover and cook for 2 to 3 minutes, or until the undersides are golden brown, and the yolks have begun to set (the egg whites won't have cooked through yet). Carefully turn the sandwiches again (some of the egg white may run off since it is still partially uncooked). Cover and cook for 1 to 3 minutes, depending on how you like your eggs. Cut the sandwiches in half diagonally and serve immediately.

NOTE: This sandwich cannot be made in a sandwich maker. It can be made on a grill if you use a skillet. If you choose to do this, follow directions for the stovetop method.

MAKES 4 SANDWICHES

FETA AND EGGPLANT ON PITA WITH SESAME-YOGURT SAUCE

This is a rather unusual grilled cheese sandwich because the cheese doesn't ooze. Instead, the feta melts into the eggplant mixture, making it wonderfully creamy and rich.

FOR THE SAUCE

1 tablespoon sesame seeds
½ cup plain yogurt or sour cream
½ teaspoon ground cumin
¼ cup loosely packed mint leaves, cut into slivers, divided
¼ teaspoon fresh lemon juice
Salt and freshly ground pepper

FOR THE FILLING

5 tablespoons olive oil
1 small onion (about ¼ pound), sliced
1 large jalapeno pepper, stemmed, seeded, and finely chopped
2 large cloves garlic, minced
1 large eggplant (about 1¼ pounds), peeled and cut into ½-inch dice
1 teaspoon toasted sesame oil
6 ounces feta cheese, cut or crumbled into pieces

2 pita breads, cut in half

To make the sauce: Heat a small skillet over low heat. Add the sesame seeds and toast, stirring occasionally, until light brown, 5 to 7 minutes (watch carefully, as the seeds can burn easily). Set aside to cool.

In a small bowl, stir together the yogurt, cumin, sesame seeds, half the mint, lemon juice, and salt and pepper to taste. Refrigerate until ready to use. (The sauce can be made 1 day in advance.)

To make the filling: Heat 2 tablespoons of the oil in a large nonstick skillet over medium heat. Add the onions and cook until they are limp but not brown, about 7 minutes. Sprinkle with salt to taste. Add the jalapeño and garlic and cook for 1 minute. Add 1 tablespoon of oil and heat for 1 minute, then reduce the heat to medium-low. Add the eggplant, stir to coat it with oil, and cover. Cook, stirring occasionally, for 30 minutes, or until the eggplant is dark brown and very soft. (Note: The eggplant may seem a little dry. Don't worry about it unless it sticks to the skillet. If this happens, add about 2 tablespoons of water, or more, as needed).

Add the sesame oil, the remaining mint, and salt to taste. Let the eggplant mixture cool *with the cover on* for 15 minutes. When still warm to the touch, check it. If it's oily, drain off the excess oil. Then stir in the feta. Transfer the filling from the skillet to a bowl. Wipe the skillet with a paper towel, but do not wash it. (The filling can be made up to 2 hours in advance and kept at room temperature. Rewarm before using.)

To assemble: Brush the remaining 2 tablespoons oil on the outside of each pita half. Carefully open each pita half to reveal the pocket, and fill with the eggplant mixture.

STOVETOP METHOD Heat the same skillet over medium-high heat for 2 minutes. Put the sandwiches in the skillet (in batches if necessary), cover, and cook for 2 minutes, or until the undersides are golden brown. Uncover, and turn the sandwiches with a spatula, pressing firmly to flatten them slightly. Cover and cook for 1 to 2 minutes more, or until the undersides are golden brown. Serve with the sauce on the side.

SANDWICH MAKER METHOD Preheat the sandwich maker. Follow directions for sandwich assembly, and cook according to the manufacturer's instructions. If your sandwich maker doesn't have an adjustable lid, be very careful when you lower the lid; if you put too much weight on the sandwiches the filling might ooze out. Serve with the sauce on the side.

GAS GRILL METHOD Brush the grill rack with oil and preheat the grill to medium-high. Follow directions for sandwich assembly. Put the sandwiches on the grill and follow directions for the stovetop method.

MAKES 4 SANDWICHES

CRAB-FETA MELT

This is a rather exotic version of the classic crab melt, featuring two kinds of cheese and a dash of curry powder to intensify the flavors. The crab mixture can be made one day in advance, making this an easy do-ahead grilled cheese sandwich.

½ pound crabmeat, preferably fresh (or canned; do not use frozen crab)

2 tablespoons mayonnaise

2 ounces feta cheese, crumbled or cut into ¼-inch dice

1 large rib celery cut into ¼-inch dice

⅓ cup fresh corn off the cob, cooked 2 minutes in boiling water (or use frozen or canned corn that has been thawed or drained)

¾ teaspoon curry powder

Freshly ground pepper

2 tablespoons butter, at room temperature

8 slices sourdough bread (¼ inch thick)

6 ounces Monterey Jack cheese, coarsely grated (or use cheddar for a sharper flavor)

In a medium bowl, stir together the crab, mayonnaise, feta, celery, corn, curry, and pepper to taste. Set aside. (The crab mixture can be made up to 1 day in advance and refrigerated. Bring to room temperature before using).

To assemble: Butter one side of each slice of bread. Place 4 slices on your work surface, buttered side down. Distribute the crab mixture evenly over the 4 slices, followed by the cheese. Place the remaining 4 bread slices on top, buttered side up.

STOVETOP METHOD Heat a large nonstick skillet over medium-high heat for 2 minutes. Put the sandwiches in the skillet (in batches if necessary), cover, and cook for 2 minutes, or until the undersides are golden brown and the cheese has begun to melt. Uncover, and turn the sandwiches with a spatula, pressing firmly to flatten them slightly. Cook for 1 minute, or until the undersides are golden brown. Turn the sandwiches again, press with the spatula, and cook for 30 seconds, or until the Monterey Jack cheese has melted completely. Let cool slightly before serving.

SANDWICH MAKER METHOD Preheat the sandwich maker. Follow directions for sandwich assembly, and cook according to the manufacturer's instructions. If your sandwich maker doesn't have an adjustable lid, be very careful when you lower the lid; if you put too much weight on the sandwiches the crab mixture might ooze out.

GAS GRILL METHOD Brush the grill rack with oil and preheat the grill to medium-high. Follow directions for sandwich assembly. Put the sandwiches on the grill and follow directions for the stovetop method.

MAKES 4 SANDWICHES

GRILLED CAPRESE

From pizza to panini, mozzarella's melting qualities and mild flavor
have made it one of our most popular cheeses. In this recipe, the
melted mozzarella creates a sweet counterpoint to the tangy tomatoes
and lemon zest, while the dry Jack cheese adds a nice nutty
component. Note that this sandwich is finished in the broiler.

> ½ cup very hot water
>
> ¼ cup (about 2 ounces) sun-dried tomatoes
>
> 6 ounces mozzarella cheese, coarsely grated
>
> 2 teaspoons grated lemon zest
>
> ½ teaspoon freshly ground pepper
>
> 3 tablespoons finely chopped fresh basil leaves, about 15
> leaves (or 2 teaspoons dried)
>
> 2 tablespoons olive oil
>
> 8 slices crusty Italian bread (¼ inch thick)
>
> 2 ounces finely grated dry Jack cheese, about ½ cup (or use
> Parmesan)

Preheat the broiler.

In a small bowl, pour the hot water over the tomatoes and let sit for
15 minutes. Drain, pat dry, and finely chop the tomatoes.

In the same bowl, toss together the tomatoes, mozzarella, lemon
zest, basil, and pepper.

To assemble: Brush one side of each slice of bread with the oil. Place
4 slices on your work surface, oiled side down. Distribute the mozzarella
mixture evenly over the 4 slices. Place the remaining 4 bread slices on
top, oiled side up, and press gently to compress the sandwiches.

STOVETOP METHOD Heat a large ovenproof skillet over medium-high heat for 2 minutes. Put the sandwiches in the skillet (in batches if necessary), cover, and cook for 2 minutes, or until the undersides are golden brown and the cheese has begun to melt. Uncover, and turn the sandwiches with a spatula, pressing firmly to flatten them slightly. Cook for 1 minute, or until the undersides are golden brown and the cheese has melted completely.

Sprinkle the dry Jack cheese over the tops of the sandwiches and transfer the skillet to the broiler. Watching carefully, broil until the cheese bubbles and browns lightly, 30 seconds to 1 minute. Serve immediately.

SANDWICH MAKER METHOD Preheat the sandwich maker. Follow directions for sandwich assembly, and cook according to the stovetop method, *except* after the initial cooking you will need to transfer the sandwiches to an ovenproof skillet for broiling and to sprinkle on the dry Jack cheese. Alternatively, you can add the dry Jack to the other ingredients and skip the broil step.

GAS GRILL METHOD Brush the grill rack with oil and preheat the grill to medium-high. Follow directions for sandwich assembly and cook according to the stovetop method, *except* after the initial cooking you will need to transfer the sandwiches to an ovenproof skillet for broiling and to sprinkle on the dry Jack. Alternatively, you can add the dry Jack to the other ingredients and skip the broil step.

MAKES 4 SANDWICHES

MODERN GRILLED CHEESE

California Grill

Italian Ham and Cheese

Garlic-Crusted Sourdough with Cheddar

Portobello and Provolone

Grilled Goat Cheese with Tapenade

Monterey Jack and Mushroom Panino

Grilled Spinach and Goat Cheese Croissant

Teleme, Orange, and Marjoram on Potato Bread

Garden Goat Cheese

Two-Cheese Mediterranean

Swiss Melt with Bacon and Artichoke Hearts

Grilled Ricotta and Shrimp with Cilantro Pesto

Smoky Southwestern Grill

CALIFORNIA GRILL

There's nothing like melting, oozing Monterey Jack cheese and creamy avocado slices to counter a spicy salsa. Try to find a salsa that's fairly thick, or, if it seems watery, drain off some of the liquid so that the bread stays crunchy.

> 2 tablespoons butter, at room temperature
> 8 slices extra-sourdough bread (¼ inch thick)
> ½ cup high-quality salsa (if using fresh, drain most of the liquid)
> 8 ounces Monterey Jack cheese, coarsely grated
> 1 large avocado (about ½ pound), cut into twelve ¼-inch-thick slices
> Salt and freshly ground pepper

To assemble: Butter one side of each slice of bread. Place 4 slices on your work surface, buttered side down. Spread the salsa on the 4 slices and distribute the cheese evenly over them. Top with the avocado slices, sprinkle with salt and pepper to taste, and place the remaining 4 bread slices on top, buttered side up.

STOVETOP METHOD Heat a large nonstick skillet over medium-high heat for 2 minutes. Put the sandwiches in the skillet (in batches if necessary), cover, and cook for 2 minutes, or until the undersides are golden brown and the cheese has begun to melt. Uncover, and turn the sandwiches with a spatula, pressing firmly to flatten them slightly. Cook for 1 minute, or until the undersides are golden brown. Turn the sandwiches again, press with the spatula, and cook for 30 seconds, or until the cheese has melted completely. Serve immediately.

Preheat the sandwich maker. Follow directions for sandwich assembly, and cook according to the manufacturer's instructions.

Brush the grill rack with oil and preheat the grill to medium-high. Follow directions for sandwich assembly. Put the sandwiches on the grill and follow directions for the stovetop method.

MAKES 4 SANDWICHES

•   •   •

ITALIAN HAM AND CHEESE

ontina cheese is rich and creamy, making it a perfect melting cheese. Although you can use the more readily available Danish Fontina, I highly recommend you seek out Italian Fontina—it's a far more flavorful cheese.

> 2 teaspoons olive oil
>
> 1 large leek (about 6 ounces), white and light green parts thinly sliced, then rinsed and patted dry
>
> ½ teaspoon kosher salt
>
> ¼ pound pancetta, cut into 4 paper-thin slices (or buy it presliced)
>
> 2 tablespoons butter, at room temperature
>
> 8 slices sourdough bread, ¼ inch thick (or for a nuttier flavor, use rye)
>
> 6 ounces Italian Fontina cheese, coarsely grated

Heat the oil in a large nonstick skillet over medium heat. Add the leeks and cook, stirring occasionally, until they are limp but not brown, about 7 minutes, then add the salt. Transfer the leeks to a bowl and let cool.

Increase the heat to medium-high and add the pancetta to the skillet. Cook for 3 minutes, or until brown. Turn and cook about 2 minutes more, or until the pancetta has turned deep golden brown. Transfer the pancetta to a plate, and when cool enough to handle, chop it into bite-size pieces. Wipe the skillet with a paper towel, but do not wash it.

To assemble: Butter one side of each slice of bread. Place 4 slices on your work surface, buttered side down. Distribute the cheese evenly over the 4 slices, followed by the leeks and pancetta. Place the remaining 4 bread slices on top, buttered side up.

STOVETOP METHOD Heat the same skillet over medium-high heat for 2 minutes. Put the sandwiches in the skillet (in batches if necessary), cover, and cook for 2 minutes, or until the undersides are golden brown and the cheese has begun to melt. Uncover, and turn the sandwiches with a spatula, pressing firmly to flatten them slightly. Cook for 1 minute, or until the undersides are golden brown. Turn the sandwiches again, press with the spatula, and cook for 30 seconds, or until the cheese has melted completely. Serve immediately.

SANDWICH MAKER METHOD Preheat the sandwich maker. Follow directions for sandwich assembly, and cook according to the manufacturer's instructions.

GAS GRILL METHOD Brush the grill rack with oil and preheat the grill to medium-high. Follow directions for sandwich assembly. Put the sandwiches on the grill and follow directions for the stovetop method.

MAKES 4 SANDWICHES

GARLIC-CRUSTED SOURDOUGH
WITH CHEDDAR

This sandwich harks back to my childhood when my friend Cheryl and I would start our Saturdays with an open-faced toasted concoction of butter, Parmesan cheese (from the green can), and garlic powder on sourdough. For this updated version, I've added cheddar cheese and substituted real garlic for garlic powder. I recommend poaching the garlic before using—to soften it and to mellow the harshness of raw garlic.

> 3 cups water
> 2 medium cloves garlic, peeled
> 2 tablespoons butter, at room temperature
> ¼ cup very finely grated Parmesan cheese (about 1 ounce)
> 8 slices sourdough bread (¼ inch thick)
> 8 ounces cheddar cheese, coarsely grated

In a saucepan, bring the water to a boil. Add the garlic, boil for 5 minutes, and drain. In a small bowl, mash the garlic with the back of a fork (or use a garlic press). Add the butter and Parmesan cheese, and mix well.

To assemble: Butter one side of each slice of bread with the garlic butter. Place 4 slices on your work surface, buttered side down. Distribute the cheddar cheese evenly over the 4 slices and top with the remaining 4 bread slices, buttered side up.

STOVETOP METHOD Heat a large nonstick skillet over medium heat for 2 minutes. Put the sandwiches in the skillet (in batches if necessary), cover, and cook for 2 to 3 minutes, or until the undersides are golden brown and the cheese has begun to melt. Uncover, and turn the sandwiches with a spatula, pressing firmly to flatten them slightly. Cook for 1 to 2 minutes, or until the undersides are golden brown. Turn the sandwiches again, press with the spatula, and cook for 30 seconds, or until the cheese has melted completely. Serve immediately.

SANDWICH MAKER METHOD Preheat the sandwich maker (if your machine has adjustable heat, set it to medium). Follow directions for sandwich assembly, and cook according to the manufacturer's instructions. Watch the sandwiches carefully, as the garlic butter on the outside of the bread can burn easily.

GAS GRILL METHOD Brush the grill rack with oil and preheat the grill to medium. Follow directions for sandwich assembly. Put the sandwiches on the grill and follow directions for the stovetop method.

MAKES 4 SANDWICHES

PORTOBELLO AND PROVOLONE

This is about as beefy as a non-meat sandwich can get—it's hearty, mushroomy, and definitely toothsome. Because there is no bread it can also be a bit messy. You may want to serve it with a knife and fork, although I enjoy eating it by hand, with plenty of napkins. This makes a great meal all by itself or with a green salad alongside.

¼ cup olive oil

3 tablespoons balsamic vinegar

Salt and freshly ground pepper

8 large portobello mushrooms (6 to 8 ounces each)

8 ounces sharp provolone cheese, coarsely grated (or use Italian Fontina)

2 ounces aged Asiago cheese, finely grated

2 teaspoons finely chopped fresh oregano (or ½ teaspoon dried)

4 slices beefsteak tomato (¼ inch thick)

Preheat the oven to 400°F.

In a small bowl, whisk together the oil, vinegar, and salt and pepper to taste. Set aside.

To prepare the mushrooms: Moisten a paper towel and wipe the mushrooms to remove dirt. Cut out the stems and the gills. Place mushrooms in a glass dish, round side up, and pour the oil mixture over them, rubbing it in with your fingers. Turn the mushrooms and lightly sprinkle the insides with salt and pepper. Marinate for 10 minutes.

To precook the mushrooms for all methods: Remove the mushrooms from marinade and place on a baking sheet, rounded side up. Bake for

10 to 12 minutes, or until they begin to brown and shrink a bit. Turn the mushrooms and bake for 10 to 12 minutes, or until some of the liquid has surfaced and the mushrooms have browned further. Remove from the oven and let sit until cool enough to handle.

To assemble: In a small bowl, mix the cheeses and oregano. Distribute the cheese mixture evenly over the inside of 4 mushroom caps, followed by a tomato slice. Sprinkle with salt and pepper to taste, and place the remaining 4 mushroom caps on top, rounded side up.

STOVETOP METHOD Heat a large nonstick skillet over medium heat for 2 minutes. Put the mushrooms in the skillet (in batches if necessary), cover, and cook for 3 to 5 minutes, or until the undersides are dark brown and the cheese has begun to melt. Uncover, and turn the mushrooms, pressing very firmly with a spatula to flatten them slightly. Cover and cook for 2 to 3 minutes or until the undersides have turned a shade or two darker and the cheese has melted completely. Let cool slightly, cut in half, and serve.

SANDWICH MAKER METHOD Preheat the sandwich maker (if your machine has adjustable heat, set it to medium). Follow directions for sandwich assembly, and cook until the grill marks are dark and the cheese has melted completely. Let cool slightly, cut in half, and serve.

GAS GRILL METHOD Brush the grill rack with oil and preheat the grill to medium. Follow directions for sandwich assembly. Grill the mushrooms for 3 to 5 minutes, or until the cheese has begun to melt (gently lift the top off one of the mushrooms to check). Turn the mushrooms with a spatula, pressing firmly to flatten them slightly, and cook 2 minutes more, or until the mushrooms are dark brown and the cheese has melted completely. Let cool slightly before serving.

MAKES 4 SANDWICHES

GRILLED GOAT CHEESE WITH TAPENADE

*W*hen hot, goat cheese takes on a quality that is almost like a cream sauce without all the calories, and paired with the olive spread called tapenade, makes a most delectable sandwich.

> 2 tablespoons butter, at room temperature
> 8 slices Italian country bread or sourdough (¼ inch thick)
> ¼ cup tapenade
> 4 ounces log-shaped fresh goat cheese, cut into 12 slices

To assemble: Butter one side of each slice of bread. Place 4 slices on your work surface, buttered side down. Spread the tapenade evenly over the 4 slices, followed by the cheese. Place the remaining 4 bread slices on top, buttered side up.

STOVETOP METHOD Heat a large nonstick skillet over medium heat for 2 minutes. Put the sandwiches in the skillet (in batches if necessary), cover, and cook for 2 to 3 minutes, or until the undersides are golden brown and the cheese has begun to soften. Uncover, and turn the sandwiches with a spatula, pressing firmly to flatten them slightly. Cover, and cook for 1 minute, or until the undersides are golden brown. Turn the sandwiches again, press with the spatula, and cook for 30 seconds, or until the cheese is soft and creamy. Serve immediately.

SANDWICH MAKER METHOD Preheat the sandwich maker (if it has adjustable heat, set it to medium). Follow directions for sandwich assembly, and cook according to the manufacturer's instructions.

GAS GRILL METHOD Brush the grill rack with oil and preheat the grill to medium. Follow directions for sandwich assembly. Put the sandwiches on the grill and follow directions for the stovetop method.

MAKES 4 SANDWICHES

MONTEREY JACK AND MUSHROOM PANINO

call this M&M for short, but it's nothing like one of America's favorite chocolate candies. Instead, it's earthy and gooey, all in one bite.

3 tablespoons olive oil
1 small yellow onion (about ¼ pound), thinly sliced
½ pound button mushroom caps, sliced ¼ inch thick
1 tablespoon chopped fresh thyme
½ teaspoon kosher salt
Freshly ground pepper
1 sweet baguette, 1 inch cut off each end
8 ounces Monterey Jack cheese, coarsely grated

Heat 1 tablespoon of the oil in a large nonstick skillet over medium heat. Add the onions and cook until they are limp but not brown, about 7 minutes. Increase the heat to medium-high, and add the mushrooms and thyme. Cook until most of the liquid has been released and cooked down, and the mushrooms are brown around the edges, about 6 minutes. Add the salt, and pepper to taste. Transfer the mixture to a bowl. Wipe the skillet with a paper towel, but do not wash the it. (The mushroom mixture may be made up to 2 hours in advance and kept covered, at room temperature. Reheat slightly before using.)

Quarter the baguette and cut each quarter in half lengthwise to make 8 pieces measuring about 5 inches. Pull out some of the center of each piece to make a trough.

To assemble: Brush the remaining 2 tablespoons oil onto the outside of each piece of bread. Place the 4 bottom pieces on your work surface, oiled side down. Distribute the mushroom mixture evenly over these pieces, followed by the cheese. You may need to press the cheese down a bit to make sure it fits. Place the remaining 4 bread pieces on top, oiled side up.

STOVETOP METHOD Heat the same skillet over medium-high heat for 2 minutes. Put the sandwiches in the skillet (in batches if necessary), and press them firmly with a spatula to flatten them slightly. Cover, and cook for 3 minutes, or until the undersides are golden brown in places and the cheese has begun to melt. Uncover, and turn the sandwiches again, pressing them very firmly to compress the bread. Cook for 2 minutes, or until the undersides are golden brown in places (the shape of the baguette prevents it from browning uniformly). Turn the sandwiches once more, pressing with the spatula, and cook for 30 seconds to 1 minute, or until the cheese has melted completely. Serve immediately.

SANDWICH MAKER METHOD Preheat the sandwich maker. Follow directions for sandwich assembly. Put the sandwiches in the machine and pull the lid down very firmly to compress them. Cook according to the manufacturer's instructions.

GAS GRILL METHOD Brush the grill rack with oil and preheat the grill to medium-high. Follow directions for sandwich assembly. Put the sandwiches on the grill and follow directions for the stovetop method.

MAKES 4 SANDWICHES

GRILLED SPINACH AND GOAT CHEESE CROISSANT

Although a croissant is not typically a bread used for grilled cheese, the copious amount of butter in this French roll makes it a natural for a cheesy filling. Just be aware that because of its high butter content and delicate texture, the croissant can burn quite easily, so watch it carefully as it cooks.

2 tablespoons butter

1 medium onion (about ½ pound), finely chopped

10 ounces spinach, stemmed, rinsed, drained and patted dry (leave a few droplets of water clinging to the leaves)

2 ounces prosciutto, chopped (optional)

3 ounces fresh goat cheese

Salt and freshly ground pepper

4 croissants, cut in half

6 ounces aged goat cheese, such as Midnight Moon, coarsely grated (or use Gruyère or Emmentaler)

Melt the butter in a large nonstick skillet over medium heat. Add the onions and cook until they are limp but not brown, about 7 minutes. Add the spinach, cover, and cook for 2 to 3 minutes, or until wilted. (If there's a lot of liquid, increase the heat to high and boil it away. You don't want a watery filling.) Add the prosciutto (if using), and fresh goat cheese and stir until cheese is melted and the prosciutto is warmed through, about 1 minute. Add salt and pepper to taste. Transfer the mixture to a dish and let it cool slightly. Wipe the skillet with a paper towel, but do not wash it.

To assemble: Distribute the spinach mixture evenly over the 4 bottom halves of the croissants, followed by the grated cheese and pepper to taste. Cover with the 4 croissant tops.

STOVETOP METHOD Heat the same skillet over medium heat for 2 minutes. Put the sandwiches in the skillet, flat side down (in batches if necessary), and press lightly with a spatula to compress the filling. Cover, and cook for 3 minutes, or until the undersides are golden brown. Uncover, and turn the sandwiches with a spatula, pressing firmly to flatten them slightly. Cover and cook for 1 to 2 minutes more, or until the undersides are golden brown and the grated cheese has melted completely. Let the sandwiches cool slightly before serving.

SANDWICH MAKER METHOD Preheat the sandwich maker (if your machine has adjustable heat, set it to medium). Follow directions for sandwich assembly, and cook according to the manufacturer's instructions. Watch carefully to be sure the croissants don't burn. Note that because of the weight of the sandwich maker, the croissants will be flattened.

GAS GRILL METHOD Although you can make this on the grill, it is a bit tricky because of the slight unwieldiness of the croissant. If you wish to try it, brush the grill rack with oil and preheat the grill to medium. Follow directions for sandwich assembly. Put the sandwiches on the grill and follow directions for the stovetop method.

MAKES 4 SANDWICHES

TELEME, ORANGE, AND MARJORAM ON POTATO BREAD

Teleme cheese is a California original, developed in the 1930s. It is thick and creamy like fresh mozzarella, and is a little bit sweet yet slightly sharp like Monterey Jack. If the Teleme is too creamy to grate, you can slice it.

> 8 ounces Teleme cheese, coarsely grated (or use mozzarella or Monterey Jack)
> 1 tablespoon grated orange peel
> 1 tablespoon finely chopped fresh marjoram
> 2 tablespoons butter, at room temperature
> 8 slices potato bread (¼ inch thick)
> 6 large slices tomato (¼ inch thick), cut in half

In a small bowl, toss the cheese, orange peel, and marjoram together.

To assemble: Butter one side of each slice of bread. Place 4 slices on your work surface, buttered side down. Distribute the cheese mixture evenly over the 4 slices, followed by the tomato slices. Place the remaining 4 bread slices on top, buttered side up.

STOVETOP METHOD Heat a large nonstick skillet over medium heat for 2 minutes. Put the sandwiches in the skillet (in batches if necessary), cover, and cook for 2 to 3 minutes, or until the undersides are golden brown and the cheese has begun to melt. Uncover, and turn the sandwiches with a spatula, pressing firmly to flatten them slightly. Cover and cook for 2 minutes, or until the undersides are golden brown. Turn the sandwiches again, press with the spatula, and cook for 30 seconds, or until the cheese has melted completely. Serve immediately.

Preheat the sandwich maker (if it has adjustable heat, set it to medium). Follow directions for sandwich assembly, and cook according to the manufacturer's instructions.

GAS GRILL METHOD Brush the grill rack with oil and preheat the grill to medium. Follow directions for sandwich assembly. Put the sandwiches on the grill and follow directions for the stovetop method.

MAKES 4 SANDWICHES

•   •   •

GARDEN GOAT CHEESE

*F*resh goat cheese takes a little longer than other cheeses to warm up and soften. Therefore, be sure to cook this sandwich on lower heat and longer, and keep it covered, as the directions indicate. Otherwise, you'll have a lukewarm sandwich.

6 ounces fresh goat cheese, at room temperature

1 teaspoon milk, or more as needed

¼ cup finely chopped green onions (white and light green parts only)

2 teaspoons finely grated lemon peel

¼ teaspoon freshly ground pepper

2 tablespoons butter, at room temperature

8 slices sourdough bread (¼ inch thick)

½ cup loosely packed watercress leaves

In a small bowl, stir together the cheese, milk, onions, lemon peel, and pepper. The mixture should be the texture of a thick frosting, not milky.

To assemble: Butter one side of each slice of bread. Place 4 slices on your work surface, buttered side down. Spread the cheese mixture evenly over the 4 slices, followed by the watercress. Place the remaining 4 bread slices on top, buttered side up.

STOVETOP METHOD Heat a large nonstick skillet over medium heat for 2 minutes. Put the sandwiches in the skillet (in batches if necessary), cover, and cook for 4 minutes, or until the undersides are golden brown and the cheese has begun to soften. Uncover, and turn the sandwiches with a spatula, pressing firmly to flatten them slightly. Cover, and cook for 2 minutes, or until the undersides are golden brown. Turn the sandwiches again, press with the spatula, and cook for 30 seconds, or until the cheese is soft and creamy. Serve immediately.

SANDWICH MAKER METHOD Preheat the sandwich maker (if your machine has adjustable heat, set it to medium). Follow directions for sandwich assembly, and cook according to the manufacturer's instructions.

GAS GRILL METHOD Brush the grill rack with oil and preheat the grill to medium. Follow directions for sandwich assembly. Put the sandwiches on the grill and follow directions for the stovetop method.

MAKES 4 SANDWICHES

TWO-CHEESE MEDITERRANEAN

*T*here's a lot going on in this sandwich, so although it says "two-cheese," it also has many other flavorful components like capers, olives, and peppers. For this reason, I particularly like this grilled cheese either as a meal or cut into smaller pieces and served as a tasty hors d'oeuvre.

2 ounces feta cheese

½ cup pitted kalamata olives, rinsed and coarsely chopped

1 tablespoon capers, drained and rinsed

1 teaspoon finely grated lemon peel

Freshly ground pepper

2 tablespoons butter, at room temperature

8 slices *pain au levain* or sourdough bread (¼ inch thick)

4 ounces Gruyère cheese, coarsely grated (or use
 Emmentaler or Monterey Jack)

4 whole roasted red peppers (from a jar), drained and cut in
 half

½ cup baby spinach leaves

In a small bowl, mix together the feta, olives, capers, lemon peel, and pepper to taste. Set aside.

To assemble: Butter one side of each slice of bread. Place 4 slices on your work surface, buttered side down. Spread the feta mixture evenly over the 4 slices. Press the Gruyére into the feta mixture, and top each slice with 2 pepper halves and the spinach. Press again to compress the filling. Place the remaining 4 bread slices on top, buttered side up.

STOVETOP METHOD Heat a large nonstick skillet over medium heat for 2 minutes. Put the sandwiches in the skillet (in batches if necessary), cover, and cook for 2 to 3 minutes, or until the undersides are golden brown and the cheese has begun to melt. Uncover, and turn the sandwiches with a spatula, pressing very firmly to flatten them slightly. Cook for 2 to 3 minutes, or until the undersides are golden brown and the spinach has wilted. Turn the sandwiches again, press with the spatula, and cook for 30 seconds, or until the Gruyère has melted completely. Serve immediately.

SANDWICH MAKER METHOD Preheat the sandwich maker (if your machine has adjustable heat, set it to medium). Follow directions for sandwich assembly, and cook according to the manufacturer's instructions.

GAS GRILL METHOD Brush the grill rack with oil and preheat the grill to medium. Follow directions for sandwich assembly. Put the sandwiches on the grill and follow directions for the stovetop method.

MAKES 4 SANDWICHES

SWISS MELT WITH BACON AND ARTICHOKE HEARTS

W*hen paired together, smoky bacon and marinated artichoke hearts are quite rich. But the addition of horseradish and tart and spicy Dijon mustard creates a nice balance while adding plenty of zip. Blanketed with onions and melted cheese, these ingredients come together to make a lively sandwich.*

> 1 tablespoon plus 1 teaspoon Dijon mustard
> 2 teaspoons prepared horseradish
> 4 slices bacon, coarsely chopped
> 1 small onion (about ¼ pound), thinly sliced
> 2 tablespoons olive oil
> 8 slices *pain au levain*, ¼-inch thick (or use sourdough or
>   hearty Italian bread)
> 1 jar (6.5 ounces) marinated artichoke hearts, drained,
>   artichokes cut into thirds lengthwise
> 6 ounces Swiss cheese, coarsely grated (or use Gruyère)

In a small bowl, stir together the mustard and horseradish.

In a large nonstick skillet, cook the bacon over medium-high heat until crisp. Drain the bacon on a plate lined with paper towels. Remove all but 1 tablespoon of the bacon grease from the skillet. Decrease the heat to medium, add the onions, and cook until they are limp and just beginning to brown on the edges, about 7 minutes. Transfer the onions to the plate with the bacon. Wipe the skillet with a paper towel, but do not wash it.

To assemble: Brush one side of each slice of bread with the oil. Place 4 slices on your work surface, oiled side down. Spread the mustard-horseradish mixture evenly on the 4 slices, then top with the artichokes, bacon, onions, and cheese (you may have to press the cheese with your palm to make it fit). Place the remaining 4 bread slices on top, oiled side up.

STOVETOP METHOD Heat the same skillet over medium-high heat for 2 minutes. Put the sandwiches in the skillet (in batches if necessary), cover, and cook for 2 minutes, or until the undersides are golden brown and the cheese has begun to melt. Uncover, and turn the sandwiches with a spatula, pressing very firmly to flatten them slightly. Cook for 1 minute, or until the undersides are golden brown. Turn the sandwiches again, press with the spatula, and cook for 30 seconds, or until the cheese has melted completely. Serve immediately.

SANDWICH MAKER METHOD Preheat the sandwich maker. Follow directions for sandwich assembly, and cook according to the manufacturer's instructions.

GAS GRILL METHOD Brush the grill rack with oil and preheat the grill to medium-high. Follow directions for sandwich assembly. Put the sandwiches on the grill and follow directions for the stovetop method.

MAKES 4 SANDWICHES

GRILLED RICOTTA AND SHRIMP WITH CILANTRO PESTO

The pecan-studded cilantro pesto makes this one of my favorite sandwiches. Not only is the pesto delicious, it's versatile as well. You can use it with the other main ingredients—creamy ricotta and shrimp—to create a satisfying pasta dish.

FOR THE PESTO

1 bunch cilantro, large stems removed
½ cup pecans, coarsely chopped
2 ounces dry Jack cheese, finely grated (or use Parmesan)
½ teaspoon salt
6 tablespoons olive oil

2 tablespoons olive oil
8 slices *pain au levain*, ¼ inch thick (or use hearty Italian or sourdough bread)
8 ounces ricotta cheese (drain if watery)
Freshly ground pepper
¼ pound cooked bay shrimp

To make the pesto: Combine the cilantro, pecans, cheese, and salt in the bowl of a food processor or blender. Process or blend until the mixture becomes pastelike. Add the 6 tablespoons oil and process until smooth (the pesto will remain somewhat chunky) and set aside. (The pesto can be made up to a day in advance and refrigerated. It may also be frozen for up to 1 month.)

To assemble: Brush one side of each slice of bread with the 2 tablespoons oil. Place 4 slices on your work surface, oiled side down. Spread the pesto evenly on the 4 slices, followed by the ricotta, pepper to taste, and the shrimp. Place the remaining 4 bread slices on top, oiled side up.

STOVETOP METHOD Heat a large nonstick skillet over medium-high heat for 2 minutes. Put the sandwiches in the skillet (in batches if necessary), cover, and cook for 2 minutes, or until the undersides are golden brown and the cheese has begun to soften. Uncover, and turn the sandwiches with a spatula, pressing firmly to flatten them slightly. Cook for 1 to 2 minutes, or until the undersides are golden brown. Turn the sandwiches again, press with the spatula, and cook for 30 seconds to 1 minute, or until the cheese is soft and creamy. Let the sandwiches cool for 5 minutes before serving.

SANDWICH MAKER METHOD Preheat the sandwich maker. Follow directions for sandwich assembly, and cook according to the manufacturer's instructions.

GAS GRILL METHOD Brush the grill rack with oil and preheat the grill to medium-high. Follow directions for sandwich assembly. Put the sandwiches on the grill and follow directions for the stovetop method.

MAKES 4 SANDWICHES

SMOKY SOUTHWESTERN GRILL

*T*his sandwich is one of my absolute favorites, and I have my friend *Diane Tegmeyer to thank for the inspiration. The recipe calls for either pasilla or Anaheim chiles; both work equally well, but pasillas are spicier and larger than the Anaheims.*

> 2 pasilla or Anaheim chiles (or use canned chiles)
>
> 8 slices bacon, coarsely chopped
>
> 4 ciabatta rolls, cut in half (or 1 loaf ciabatta cut into 3-inch-wide sections, or use any type of Italian bread)
>
> 2 tablespoons olive oil
>
> 12 ounces mozzarella, coarsely grated (if watery, drain slightly and cut into thin slices rather than grate it)
>
> 4 ounces fresh goat cheese, crumbled or pinched into pea-size pieces
>
> 4 large slices tomato, ¼ inch thick

To roast the peppers: Preheat the broiler. Or, if you have a gas stove, turn on one burner. Place the chiles under the broiler or, if using a gas burner, hold one chile with tongs over the flame. Cook, turning frequently, until skin is charred all over. Repeat with the remaining chile. Place the chiles in a resealable plastic bag and set aside for 20 minutes. Using a small sharp knife, scrape off the charred skin, cut off the stems, then cut the chiles into ½-inch-wide strips. Set aside.

Meanwhile, in a large nonstick skillet, cook the bacon over medium-high heat until crispy. Drain on paper towels. Wipe the skillet with a paper towel, but do not wash it.

To assemble: Pull out some of the center of each roll to create a well. Brush the outside of each roll with the oil. Place the 4 bottom

pieces on your work surface, oiled side down. Distribute the mozzarella evenly over these pieces, followed by the bacon, chiles, tomatoes, and goat cheese. Place the remaining 4 pieces of bread on top, oiled side up.

STOVETOP METHOD Heat the same skillet over medium heat for 2 minutes. Put the sandwiches in the skillet (in batches if necessary) and press firmly with a spatula to flatten them slightly. Cover and cook for 3 to 4 minutes, or until the undersides are golden brown in places and the mozzarella has begun to melt. Uncover, and turn the sandwiches with the spatula, pressing very firmly. Cover, and cook for 2 to 3 minutes, or until the undersides are golden brown in places (the shape of the roll prevents uniform browning). Turn the sandwiches again, press with the spatula, and cook for 30 seconds to 1 minute, or until the mozzarella has melted completely. Serve immediately.

SANDWICH MAKER METHOD Preheat the sandwich maker (if it has adjustable heat, set it to medium). Follow directions for sandwich assembly. Put the sandwiches in the machine and pull the lid down very firmly to compress them. Cook according to the manufacturer's instructions.

GAS GRILL METHOD Brush the grill rack with oil and preheat the grill to medium. Follow directions for sandwich assembly. Put the sandwiches on the grill, cover, and cook for 4 to 5 minutes (3 to 4 minutes if using bread slices) or until the undersides have distinct grill marks and the mozzarella has begun to melt. Turn carefully with a spatula, pressing very firmly to compress the rolls. Cover and cook about 4 minutes (2 to 3 minutes if using bread slices) or until the undersides have distinct grill marks. Turn again and cook for 1 minute, or until the mozzarella has melted completely.

MAKES 4 SANDWICHES

SEASONAL GRILLED CHEESE

Grilled Cheddar and Broccoli with Cayenne Butter

Swiss Cheese with Swiss Chard

Buttery Fig and Blue Cheese Melt

Tomato, Tarragon, and Goat Cheese on Olive Bread

Fresh Cheese and Herbs on Italian Bread

Summer Plums with Brie and Blue Cheese

Taleggio with Rosemary Grapes on Focaccia

GRILLED CHEDDAR AND BROCCOLI WITH CAYENNE BUTTER

*I*n the winter, when cruciferous vegetables such as broccoli, cauliflower, and Brussels sprouts are at their best, it makes sense to showcase them. This is a take on the classic broccoli-cheddar soup, but much easier and, in my opinion, much better!

$\frac{1}{2}$ pound broccoli crowns
1$\frac{1}{2}$ quarts (6 cups) water
1 teaspoon salt
2 tablespoons plus 1 teaspoon butter, at room temperature
$\frac{1}{4}$ cup sliced almonds (about 1 ounce)
$\frac{1}{2}$ teaspoon cayenne pepper
8 slices whole wheat or sourdough bread ($\frac{1}{4}$ inch thick)
8 ounces best-quality cheddar cheese, coarsely grated

Bring the water to a boil in a medium-size pot. Separate the broccoli into florets measuring about 2 inches long and 1$\frac{1}{2}$ inches wide. Add the salt and broccoli and cook until the broccoli is bright green and still firm but slightly tender when pierced with a fork, about 3 minutes (the broccoli will not be cooked all the way through). Drain and let it sit just until cool enough to handle. Cut florets into halves or quarters, to create pieces that aren't too bulky. You should end up with about 20 pieces. Set aside.

In a large nonstick skillet, melt 1 teaspoon butter over medium heat. Add the almonds and cook, stirring occasionally, until they are toasted, about 4 minutes. Transfer the almonds to a bowl. Wipe the skillet with a paper towel, but do not wash it.

In a small bowl, mash the remaining 2 tablespoons butter and cayenne pepper together until blended.

To assemble: Butter one side of each slice of bread with the cayenne butter. Place 4 slices on your work surface, buttered side down. Distribute the broccoli evenly over the 4 slices, followed by the cheese (you may have to press the cheese in place with your hand). Sprinkle the almonds over the cheese. Place the remaining 4 bread slices on top, buttered side up.

STOVETOP METHOD Heat the same skillet over medium heat for 2 minutes. Put the sandwiches in the skillet (in batches if necessary), cover, and cook for 2 to 3 minutes, or until the undersides are golden brown and the cheese has begun to melt. Uncover, and turn the sandwiches with a spatula, pressing firmly to flatten them slightly. Cover, and cook for 1 minute, or until the undersides are golden brown. Turn the sandwiches again, press with the spatula, and cook for 30 seconds, or until the cheese has melted completely. Serve immediately.

SANDWICH MAKER METHOD Preheat the sandwich maker (if your machine has adjustable heat, set it to medium). Follow directions for sandwich assembly, and cook according to the manufacturer's instructions. Watch the sandwiches carefully, as the cayenne butter can burn easily.

GAS GRILL METHOD Brush the grill rack with oil and preheat the grill to medium. Follow directions for sandwich assembly. Put the sandwiches on the grill and follow directions for the stovetop method.

MAKES 4 SANDWICHES

SWISS CHEESE WITH SWISS CHARD

This sandwich puts a rather forlorn wintertime vegetable to great use. The somewhat bitter Swiss chard comes alive with the sweet currants and the heat of the red pepper flakes.

1 tablespoon currants
3 tablespoons olive oil
1 small onion (about ¼ pound), finely chopped
1 bunch Swiss chard (about 1 pound), washed and drained
    slightly (leave some water on the leaves)
1 tablespoon red wine vinegar
½ teaspoon red pepper flakes
Salt
4 ciabatta rolls or 1 loaf ciabatta cut into four 3-inch-wide
    pieces, cut in half (or use hearty Italian bread or
    sourdough cut ¼ inch thick)
6 ounces Swiss cheese, coarsely grated

Place the currants in a small heatproof bowl. Pour hot water over them and let soak for 10 minutes, or until they are soft and a little plump. Drain and set aside.

Cut the thick stems off the chard and cut the leaves roughly into 2-inch pieces.

In a large nonstick skillet, heat 1 tablespoon of the oil over medium heat. Add the onions and cook, stirring occasionally, until they are limp but not brown, about 7 minutes. Add the chard, cover, and cook until it is wilted and very tender, 7 to 9 minutes. (If it looks dry, add water 1 tablespoon at a time.) Increase the heat to medium-high and add the vinegar. Cook until the vinegar aroma dissipates, about 1 minute. Add the currants, pepper flakes, and salt to taste, and mix well. Transfer the mixture to a plate to cool slightly. Wipe out the skillet but do not wash it. (The chard mixture can be made up to 2 hours in advance. Cover and keep at room temperature. Warm it before using.)

To assemble: Brush the outside of the rolls with the remaining 2 tablespoons of oil. Place the 4 bottom pieces on your work surface, oiled side down. Distribute the chard mixture evenly over the 4 pieces, followed by the cheese. Place the remaining 4 pieces of ciabatta on top, oiled side up.

STOVETOP METHOD Heat the same skillet over medium heat for 2 minutes. Put the sandwiches in the skillet (in batches if necessary), and press firmly with a spatula to flatten. Cover, and cook for 3 minutes, or until undersides are golden brown in places and cheese has begun to melt. Uncover, and turn the sandwiches with the spatula, pressing very firmly to compress the roll. Cook for 2 minutes, or until the undersides are golden brown in places. Turn again, press with spatula, and cook for 30 seconds to 1 minute, or until cheese has melted completely. Serve immediately.

SANDWICH MAKER METHOD Preheat the sandwich maker (if it has adjustable heat, set it to medium). Follow directions for sandwich assembly. Put the sandwiches in the machine and pull the lid down very firmly to compress them. Cook according to the manufacturer's instructions.

GAS GRILL METHOD Brush grill rack with oil and preheat grill to medium. Follow directions for sandwich assembly. Grill the sandwiches, covered, for 4 to 5 minutes (3 to 4 minutes if using bread slices) or until undersides have distinct grill marks and cheese has begun to melt. Turn carefully with a spatula, pressing very firmly. Cover and cook about 4 minutes (2 to 3 minutes if using bread slices) or until the undersides have distinct grill marks. Turn again and cook for 1 minute, or until cheese has melted completely.

MAKES 4 SANDWICHES

BUTTERY FIG AND BLUE CHEESE MELT

This is a simple sandwich that takes advantage of the two short but sweet fig seasons—the first in early summer and the second in early fall. Putting figs and blue cheese in the same sandwich took little thought; it's a classic combination. However, the buttery, creamy results were anything but predictable. Wow.

> 3 tablespoons unsalted butter, at room temperature
> 6 ripe but firm fresh figs, stemmed and cut in half lengthwise
> 8 slices crusty Italian bread (¼ inch thick)
> 4 ounces creamy-style blue cheese, such as Gorgonzola or
>   Point Reyes Blue (do not use pre-crumbled blue cheese),
>   at room temperature

In a large nonstick skillet, melt 1 tablespoon of the butter over medium-high heat. Place the figs cut-side down and sauté until they are golden around the edges and pillow-soft to the touch, about 2 minutes. Turn and cook for 1 minute more. Transfer to a plate and let cool slightly. Wipe out the skillet with a paper towel and set aside.

To assemble: Butter one side of each slice of bread with the remaining 2 tablespoons butter. Place 4 slices on your work surface, buttered side down. Spread the cheese evenly over the 4 slices, followed by the figs. Place the remaining 4 bread slices on top, buttered side up.

STOVETOP METHOD Heat the same skillet over medium-high heat for 2 minutes. Put the sandwiches in the skillet (in batches if necessary), cover, and cook for 2 minutes, or until the undersides are golden brown and the cheese has begun to melt. Uncover, and turn the sandwiches with a spatula, pressing firmly to flatten them slightly. Cook for

1 minute, or until the undersides are golden brown. Turn the sandwiches again, press with the spatula, and cook for 30 seconds, or until the cheese has melted completely. Serve immediately.

SANDWICH MAKER METHOD Preheat the sandwich maker. Follow directions for sandwich assembly, and cook according to the manufacturer's instructions.

GAS GRILL METHOD Brush the grill rack with oil and preheat the grill to medium-high. Follow directions for sandwich assembly. Put the sandwiches on the grill and follow directions for the stovetop method.

VARIATION: If you're interested in adding an herbaceous note to this sandwich, take 1 tablespoon fresh rosemary (or 1 teaspoon dried rosemary) chop it, and mix it into the cheese before spreading on the bread.

MAKES 4 SANDWICHES

TOMATO, TARRAGON, AND GOAT CHEESE ON OLIVE BREAD

The combination of tarragon, tomato, and goat cheese has to be tried to be believed—it is truly magnificent. The olive bread completes the fresh, herbaceous taste of the filling. If you cannot find olive bread, you can add chopped olives to the filling.

> 6 ounces fresh goat cheese
> 1 small shallot, finely chopped
> 1 small tomato (about 4 ounces), seeded and cut into ¼-inch
>   dice
> 1 tablespoon chopped fresh tarragon (or use 1½ teaspoons
>   dried)
> 8 slices olive bread ¼ inch thick (or use sourdough or hearty
>   Italian bread)
> 2 tablespoons olive oil

In a small bowl, stir together the cheese, shallot, tomato, and tarragon.

To assemble: Brush one side of each slice of bread with the oil. Place 4 slices on your work surface, oiled side down. Spread the cheese mixture evenly over the 4 slices. Place the remaining 4 bread slices on top, oiled side up.

STOVETOP METHOD Heat a large nonstick skillet over medium-high heat for 2 minutes. Put the sandwiches in the skillet (in batches if necessary), cover, and cook for 2 minutes, or until the undersides are golden brown and the cheese has begun to soften. Uncover, and turn the sandwiches with a spatula, pressing firmly to flatten them slightly. Cook for 1 minute, or until the undersides are golden brown. Turn the sandwiches again, press with the spatula, and cook for 30 seconds, or until the cheese is soft and creamy. Serve immediately.

SANDWICH MAKER METHOD Preheat the sandwich maker. Follow directions for sandwich assembly, and cook according to the manufacturer's instructions.

GAS GRILL METHOD Brush the grill rack with oil and preheat the grill to medium-high. Follow directions for sandwich assembly. Put the sandwiches on the grill and follow directions for the stovetop method.

MAKES 4 SANDWICHES

•   •   •

FRESH CHEESE AND HERBS ON ITALIAN BREAD

*F*romage blanc is a fresh cheese that tastes like a cross between cottage cheese and ricotta cheese, with a little sour cream thrown in. It has an earthy quality that blends beautifully with the fresh herbs in this sandwich. If you can't find fromage blanc, use ricotta instead.*

8 ounces fromage blanc, at room temperature

2 tablespoons finely chopped fresh mint

2 tablespoons finely chopped fresh chives

1½ teaspoons finely chopped fresh rosemary (or use
    ¾ teaspoon dried)

Freshly ground pepper

8 slices hearty Italian bread (¼ inch thick)

2 tablespoons olive oil

In a medium bowl stir together the cheese, mint, chives, rosemary, and pepper to taste.

To assemble: Brush one side of each slice of bread with the oil. Place 4 slices on your work surface, oiled side down. Spread the cheese mixture evenly over the 4 slices. Place the remaining 4 bread slices on top, oiled side up.

STOVETOP METHOD Heat a large nonstick skillet over medium heat for 2 minutes. Put the sandwiches in the skillet (in batches if necessary), cover, and cook for 2 to 3 minutes, or until the undersides are golden brown and the cheese has begun to soften. Uncover, and turn the sandwiches with a spatula, pressing firmly to flatten them slightly. Cover and cook for 1 minute, or until the undersides are golden brown. Turn the sandwiches again, press with the spatula, and cook for 30 seconds, or until the cheese is soft and creamy. Serve immediately.

SANDWICH MAKER METHOD Preheat the sandwich maker (if your machine has adjustable heat, set it to medium). Follow directions for sandwich assembly, and cook according to the manufacturer's instructions.

GAS GRILL METHOD Brush the grill rack with oil and preheat the grill to medium. Follow directions for sandwich assembly. Put the sandwiches on the grill and follow directions for the stovetop method.

MAKES 4 SANDWICHES

SUMMER PLUMS WITH BRIE AND BLUE CHEESE

The combination of creamy Brie with pungent blue cheese can't be beat. The addition of one of the best fruits of summer creates a lovely sweet-tart balance, and the arugula adds a peppery component. If you want to mix things up, you can also add a slice of prosciutto to each sandwich, making it richer and a bit saltier.

2 tablespoons butter, at room temperature

8 slices sourdough bread (¼ inch thick)

2 large plums, each cut into twelve ¼-inch slices

6 ounces Brie cheese, rind removed; cut into 12 pieces

2 ounces creamy-style blue cheese (such as Maytag), pinched or crumbled into small pieces

1 cup arugula leaves

To assemble: Butter one side of each slice of bread. Place 4 slices on your work surface, buttered side down. Distribute the plums evenly over the 4 slices, followed by the Brie, blue cheese, and arugula. Place the remaining 4 bread slices on top, buttered side up.

STOVETOP METHOD Heat a large nonstick skillet over medium-high heat for 2 minutes. Put the sandwiches in the skillet (in batches if necessary), cover, and cook for 2 minutes, or until the undersides are golden brown and the cheese has begun to melt. Uncover, and turn the sandwiches with a spatula, pressing firmly to flatten them slightly. Cook for 1 to 2 minutes more, or until the undersides are golden brown. Turn the sandwiches again, press with the spatula, and cook for 30 seconds, or until the cheese has melted completely. Serve immediately.

SANDWICH MAKER METHOD Preheat the sandwich maker. Follow directions for sandwich assembly, and cook according to the manufacturer's instructions.

GAS GRILL METHOD Brush the grill rack with oil and preheat the grill to medium-high. Follow directions for sandwich assembly. Put the sandwiches on the grill and follow directions for the stovetop method.

MAKES 4 SANDWICHES

TALEGGIO WITH ROSEMARY GRAPES ON FOCACCIA

Although this recipe calls for plain focaccia, sometimes this Italian flat bread can be hard to find. If you can't find the plain version, then use herbed focaccia or simply use Italian-style rolls, such as ciabatta. Taleggio is a creamy and pungent Italian cheese that can be found in cheese shops and many grocery stores. If you can't find it, use Camembert or any flavorful creamy cheese.

3 tablespoons olive oil

½ cup seedless red grapes, cut in half lengthwise

2 teaspoons finely chopped fresh rosemary (or use ¾ teaspoon dried)

Salt and freshly ground pepper

4 pieces plain focaccia (about 4-by-4 inches), cut in half (or use ciabatta rolls or 8 slices hearty Italian bread, ¼ inch thick)

8 ounces Taleggio or other creamy washed-rind cheese such as Red Hawk (or use Camembert and remove the rind), cut into 12 slices

Heat 1 tablespoon of the oil in a large nonstick skillet over medium heat. Add the grapes and rosemary and cook, stirring constantly, until the grapes begin to brown and one or two of the skins start to slip off, 4 to 5 minutes. Add salt and pepper to taste. Transfer the grapes to a bowl. Wipe the skillet with a paper towel, but do not wash it.

To assemble: Pull out some of the center of each piece of bread to create a well. Brush the outside of each piece with the remaining

2 tablespoons oil. Place the 4 bottom pieces on your work surface, oiled side down. Distribute the cheese evenly over the 4 pieces, followed by the grapes. Place the remaining 4 bread pieces on top, oiled side up.

STOVETOP METHOD Heat the same skillet over medium-high heat for 2 minutes. Put the sandwiches in the skillet (in batches if necessary), cover, and cook for 2 to 3 minutes, or until the bread has turned a shade darker and the cheese has begun to melt. Uncover, and turn the sandwiches with a spatula, pressing very firmly to compress them. Cook for 2 to 3 minutes more, or until the undersides are golden brown. Turn the sandwiches again, press with the spatula, and cook for 1 minute, or until the cheese has melted completely. Serve immediately.

SANDWICH MAKER METHOD Preheat the sandwich maker. Follow directions for sandwich assembly, and cook according to the manufacturer's instructions.

GAS GRILL METHOD Brush the grill rack with oil and preheat the grill to medium-high. Follow directions for sandwich assembly. Put the sandwiches on the grill and follow directions for the stovetop method.

MAKES 4 SANDWICHES

QUESADILLAS

Smoked Salmon and Brie Quesadilla

Oaxaca Cheese, Chorizo, and Shrimp Quesadilla

Spanish Quesadilla with Smoky Crème Fraîche

Black Bean, Zucchini, and Monterey Jack Quesadilla

Butternut Squash and Blue Cheese Quesadilla

SMOKED SALMON AND BRIE QUESADILLA

The combination of Brie and cream cheese ensures that this quesadilla falls under the category of "rich," and the addition of smoked salmon seals the deal. Because of its full flavors, this not only makes a hearty meal, but also works well as an hors d'oeuvre when cut into small wedges.

4 ounces cream cheese, at room temperature
2 tablespoons minced red onion
1 tablespoon plus 1 teaspoon capers, drained
1 teaspoon lemon juice
¼ teaspoon freshly ground pepper
2 tablespoons butter, at room temperature
4 large (9- to 10-inch) flour tortillas
8 ounces Brie cheese, rind removed; cheese cut into 8 slices
    (or 8 pieces if the cheese is quite soft)
¼ pound smoked salmon, thinly sliced

In a small bowl, mix together the cream cheese, onions, capers, lemon juice, and pepper.

To assemble: Butter one side of each tortilla and place them on your work surface, buttered side down. Spread the cream cheese mixture evenly over each tortilla. Place 2 slices of cheese on the bottom half of each tortilla. Fold the tortillas in half to enclose the filling, forming a half-moon.

STOVETOP METHOD Heat a large nonstick skillet over medium-high heat for 2 minutes. Place 2 of the quesadillas in the skillet, cover, and cook for 2 minutes or until the undersides are golden brown and the cheese has begun to melt. Uncover, and turn the quesadillas with a spatula. Cover and cook for about 1 minute, or until the undersides are golden brown and the cheese has melted completely. Remove from the skillet, gently pull the quesadillas apart and place one quarter of the salmon slices inside each one. Repeat with the remaining 2 quesadillas. Cut the quesadillas in half (or in smaller wedges), and serve immediately.

SANDWICH MAKER METHOD Preheat the sandwich maker. Follow directions for quesadilla assembly, and cook according to the manufacturer's instructions. The quesadillas will take about 3 to 4 minutes to cook. Unless you have a large sandwich maker, you will have to cook the quesadillas in batches.

GAS GRILL METHOD Brush the grill rack with oil and preheat the grill to medium-high. Follow directions for quesadilla assembly above. Put the quesadillas on the grill and follow directions for the stovetop method.

MAKES 4 QUESADILLAS

OAXACA CHEESE, CHORIZO, AND SHRIMP QUESADILLA

first made this quesadilla for some friends who'd gathered around my stove during recipe-testing time. They went wild for it, so I knew I didn't need to change a thing. The sublime combination of shellfish and sausage is undisputed, and enhanced with melted cheese it's unbeatable.

¼ pound Spanish chorizo sausage, cut into ¼-inch-thick slices (or use linguiça or andouille)
1 large yellow onion (about ¾ pound), thinly sliced
20 medium shrimp (about 6 ounces of 41–50 count), shelled and deveined
Salt
8 ounces Oaxaca cheese, coarsely grated (or use mozzarella; if watery, cut it into thin slices)
4 large (9- to 10-inch) flour tortillas
2 tablespoons olive or vegetable oil

In a large nonstick skillet, cook the chorizo over medium heat, stirring occasionally, until it turns a shade or two darker and much of the fat has been rendered, 8 to 10 minutes. Transfer the chorizo to a plate lined with paper towels. Discard all but 1 tablespoon of the fat left in the skillet.

Use the same skillet to cook the onions over medium heat, stirring occasionally until they are limp and golden, but not brown, 7 to 9 minutes. Increase the heat to medium-high and add the shrimp. If the skillet seems dry, add 1 to 2 teaspoons of olive oil. Cook until the shrimp turn a vibrant pink and feel fairly firm to the touch, about 2 minutes. Add salt to taste. Transfer the shrimp mixture to a plate. Wipe the skillet with a paper towel, but do not wash it.

To assemble: Brush one side of each tortilla with oil and place them on your work surface, oiled side down. Distribute the chorizo slices evenly over the bottom half of each tortilla, followed by the shrimp mixture and the cheese. Fold the tortillas in half to enclose the filling, forming a half-moon.

STOVETOP METHOD Heat the same skillet over medium-high heat for 2 minutes. Place 2 of the quesadillas in the skillet, cover, and cook for 2 minutes or until the undersides are golden brown and the cheese has begun to melt. Uncover, and turn the quesadillas with a spatula. Cook for 1 to 2 minutes, or until the undersides are golden brown and the cheese has melted completely. Repeat with the remaining 2 quesadillas. Cut the quesadillas in half, and serve immediately.

SANDWICH MAKER METHOD Preheat the sandwich maker. Follow directions for quesadilla assembly, and cook according to the manufacturer's instructions. The quesadillas will take about 3 to 4 minutes to cook. Unless you have a large sandwich maker, you will have to cook the quesadillas in batches.

GAS GRILL METHOD Brush the grill rack with oil and preheat the grill to medium-high. Follow directions for quesadilla assembly. Put the quesadillas on the grill and follow directions for the stovetop method.

MAKES 4 QUESADILLAS

SPANISH QUESADILLA WITH SMOKY CRÈME FRAÎCHE

*T*he white anchovies in this recipe are worth searching for. However, if you can't find them, use canned anchovies and be sure to rinse them first. If you're not an anchovy fan, you can substitute good-quality olives instead.

¼ cup (2 ounces) crème fraîche

½ teaspoon Spanish hot smoked paprika (see note), or use Hungarian hot paprika

4 large (9- to 10-inch) flour tortillas

2 tablespoons olive or vegetable oil

8 ounces Manchego cheese, coarsely grated (or use Monterey Jack)

4 white anchovies, also called boquerones, cut in half (or use ½ cup sliced kalamata olives)

8 pequillo peppers, slit down one side and opened (see note, or use roasted red peppers)

In a small bowl, mix together the crème fraîche and paprika. Set aside. (This can be made up to a day in advance and refrigerated.)

To assemble: Brush one side of each tortilla with the oil and place them on your work surface, oiled side down. Distribute the cheese evenly over the bottom half of each tortilla, followed by 2 anchovy pieces and 2 peppers. Fold the tortillas in half to enclose the filling, forming a half-moon.

STOVETOP METHOD Heat a large nonstick skillet over medium-high heat for 2 minutes. Place 2 of the quesadillas in the skillet, cover, and cook for 2 minutes or until the undersides are golden brown and the cheese has begun to melt. Uncover, and turn the quesadillas with a spatula. Cook for 1 to 2 minutes, or until the undersides are golden brown and the cheese has melted completely. Repeat with the remaining 2 quesadillas. Cut the quesadillas in half, and serve immediately.

SANDWICH MAKER METHOD Preheat the sandwich maker. Follow directions for quesadilla assembly, and cook according to the manufacturer's instructions. The quesadillas will take about 3 to 4 minutes to cook. Unless you have a large sandwich maker, you will probably have to cook the quesadillas in batches.

GAS GRILL METHOD Brush the grill rack with oil and preheat the grill to medium-high. Follow directions for quesadilla assembly. Put the quesadillas on the grill and follow directions for the stovetop method.

NOTE: Smoky Spanish paprika and pequillo peppers can be found at many specialty grocery stores. Or you can order them from the Spanish Table website: www.spanishtable.com.

MAKES 4 QUESADILLAS

BLACK BEAN, ZUCCHINI, AND MONTEREY JACK QUESADILLA

The ricotta cheese in this delectable quesadilla serves a dual purpose: it binds the filling so that the beans and zucchini don't spill out, and it adds its characteristic creamy flavor. The melted Jack cheese doubles that effect.

¼ cup olive oil
1 medium yellow onion (about ½ pound), finely chopped
3 medium zucchini (about 12 ounces) cut into ¼-inch dice
1 large jalapeño chile, stemmed, seeded, and minced
⅓ cup canned black beans, drained
¼ cup finely chopped fresh oregano leaves (or use 1
    tablespoon dried)
2 tablespoons red wine vinegar
1 teaspoon salt (or more to taste)
¼ cup ricotta cheese (drain if watery)
4 large (9- to 10-inch) flour tortillas
8 ounces Monterey Jack cheese, coarsely grated
½ cup crème fraîche, sour cream, or Mexican crema
    (optional)

In a large nonstick skillet, heat 2 tablespoons of the oil over medium heat. Add the onions and cook until they begin to soften but not brown, about 5 minutes. Add the zucchini and jalapeño and cook, stirring occasionally, 8 to 10 minutes, or until the zucchini is soft but still holding its shape. Add the beans, oregano, vinegar, and salt, and stir well. Remove the skillet from the heat and let cool 5 minutes. Add the ricotta and stir well. Transfer the mixture to a plate. Wipe the skillet with a paper towel but do not wash it.

To assemble: Brush one side of each tortilla with the remaining 2 tablespoons oil and place the tortillas on your work surface, oiled side down. Distribute the Jack cheese evenly over the bottom half of each tortilla, followed by the zucchini mixture. Fold the tortillas in half to enclose the filling, forming a half-moon.

STOVETOP METHOD Heat the same skillet over medium-high heat for 2 minutes. Place 2 of the quesadillas in the skillet, cover, and cook for 2 minutes or until the undersides are golden brown and the cheese has begun to melt. Uncover, and turn the quesadillas with a spatula. Cook for 1 to 2 minutes, or until the undersides are golden brown and the cheese has melted completely. Repeat with the remaining 2 quesadillas. To serve, cut the quesadillas in half, drizzle with the créme fraîche if using, and serve immediately

SANDWICH MAKER METHOD Preheat the sandwich maker. Follow directions for quesadilla assembly, and cook according to the manufacturer's instructions. The quesadillas will take about 3 to 4 minutes to cook. Unless you have a large sandwich maker, you will probably have to cook the quesadillas in batches.

GAS GRILL METHOD Brush the grill rack with oil and preheat the grill to medium-high. Follow directions for quesadilla assembly. Put the quesadillas on the grill and follow directions for the stovetop method.

MAKES 4 QUESADILLAS

BUTTERNUT SQUASH AND BLUE CHEESE QUESADILLA

This quesadilla has three cheeses in it: the Parmesan lends a nuttiness and crunchiness to the exterior, the Gruyère gives it a seductive creaminess, and the blue cheese provides a pungent contrast to the sweet squash. It's a hearty combination that is perfect for autumn when butternut squash makes its annual debut.

1 small butternut squash (about 1 pound), peeled, seeded, and cut in half lengthwise

1 tablespoon olive oil

Salt and freshly ground pepper

2 tablespoons butter, at room temperature

¼ cup finely grated Parmesan cheese

4 large (9- to 10-inch) flour tortillas

8 ounces Gruyère cheese, coarsely grated (or use Emmentaler or Fontina)

4 ounces blue cheese, crumbled

2 tablespoons finely chopped fresh sage (or use 2 teaspoons dried)

Preheat the oven to 400°F. Line a baking sheet with parchment paper. Cut each squash half crosswise into ¼ inch slices, resembling half-moons. In a large bowl, toss the squash with the olive oil, and sprinkle with salt and pepper to taste. Place the squash on the prepared baking sheet and roast for 20 to 25 minutes, turning the pieces over halfway through, or until the squash feels soft when pierced with a fork and the slices are slightly caramelized. Set aside to cool slightly.

In a small bowl, mash the butter and Parmesan together.

To assemble: Spread the Parmesan butter on one side of each tortilla and place them on your work surface, buttered side down. Place 6 slices of squash on the bottom half of each tortilla, followed by the Gruyére, blue cheese, and sage. Fold the tortillas in half to enclose the filling, forming a half-moon. (You may have extra squash slices; save for another use or enjoy as a snack.)

STOVETOP METHOD Heat a large nonstick skillet over medium heat for 2 minutes. Place 2 of the quesadillas in the skillet, cover, and cook for 2 minutes or until the undersides are golden brown and the cheese has begun to melt. Watch carefully, as the Parmesan butter can burn easily. Uncover, and turn the quesadillas with a spatula. Cook for about 1 minute, or until the undersides are golden brown and the cheese has melted completely. Repeat with the remaining 2 quesadillas. Cut the quesadillas in half, and serve immediately.

SANDWICH MAKER METHOD Preheat the sandwich maker (if your machine has adjustable heat, set it to medium). Follow directions for quesadilla assembly. Cook for 3 to 4 minutes or until the cheese has melted completely. Watch carefully, as the Parmesan butter can burn easily. Unless you have a large sandwich maker, you will have to cook the quesadillas in batches.

GAS GRILL METHOD Brush the grill rack with oil and preheat the grill to medium. Follow directions for quesadilla assembly. Put the quesadillas on the grill and follow directions for the stovetop method.

MAKES 4 QUESADILLAS

SWEET GRILLED CHEESE

Grilled Brie with Apricot Jam

Hawaiian Grilled Cheese

Chocolate-Hazelnut and Goat Cheese Melt

Creamy Chocolate and Pear

Ricotta and Marmalade with Chocolate Sauce

Rich Raspberry Brioche

Goat Cheese and Honey on Cinnamon-Raisin Bread

Nectarines, Blueberries, and Ricotta on Egg Bread

GRILLED BRIE WITH APRICOT JAM

*W*ith just a few ingredients, this sandwich is as easy as it is elegant. It also lends itself to all types of variations. You don't like apricot jam? Then use strawberry, fig, or any type of jam you like. You want to use a triple-cream Brie instead of a single-cream style? Go right ahead and boost the richness factor. This is your sandwich to customize and enjoy. (Note that it is easiest to remove the rind and slice Brie when the cheese is cold. Bring the cheese to room temperature before using.)

> 1 sweet baguette,1 inch cut off each end
>
> 4 tablespoons unsalted butter, melted
>
> 2 tablespoons plus 2 teaspoons apricot jam
>
> 6 ounces Brie cheese, rind removed; cut into 12 slices

Quarter the baguette and cut each piece in half lengthwise to make 8 pieces measuring about 5 inches long. Pull out some of the center of each piece of bread to create a trough.

To assemble: Brush the outside of each piece of bread with the melted butter. Place the 4 bottom pieces on your work surface, buttered side down. Spread the jam evenly over the 4 pieces, and distribute the cheese on top of the jam. Place the remaining 4 baguette pieces on top, buttered side up.

STOVETOP METHOD Heat a large nonstick skillet over medium-high heat for 2 minutes. Put the sandwiches in the skillet (in batches if necessary), cover, and cook for 3 minutes, or until the undersides are golden brown in places and the cheese has begun to melt. Uncover, and turn the sandwiches again, pressing them very firmly to compress the bread. Cook for 2 minutes, or until the undersides are golden brown in places. (The shape of the baguette prevents it from browning uniformly.) Turn the sandwiches once more, pressing with the spatula, and cook for 30 seconds to 1 minute, or until the cheese has melted completely. Serve immediately.

SANDWICH MAKER METHOD Preheat the sandwich maker. Follow directions for sandwich assembly, and cook according to the manufacturer's instructions.

GAS GRILL METHOD Brush the grill rack with oil and preheat the grill to medium-high. Follow directions for sandwich assembly. Put the sandwiches on the grill and follow directions for the stovetop method.

MAKES 4 SANDWICHES

HAWAIIAN GRILLED CHEESE

With *fresh pineapple and toasted coconut, this sandwich offers a taste of Hawaii between two slices of bread. The recipe calls for Hawaiian bread, which is a very sweet, airy bread, similar to egg bread. If you can't find it, then substitute egg bread and double the sugar. Note that this sandwich is cooked at a lower temperature, which helps prevent the delicate bread from burning.*

¼ cup sweetened coconut

8 ounces fromage blanc (or use ricotta, preferably whole milk; drain if watery)

½ cup finely diced fresh pineapple (or used canned, drained pineapple) plus extra for garnish

2 tablespoons sugar (¼ cup if using egg bread)

8 slices Hawaiian bread (if using a large round rather than pre-sliced loaf, cut four ½-inch slices from widest part of loaf and cut slices in half), or use egg bread

2 tablespoons unsalted butter, at room temperature

Preheat the oven to 300°F.

Spread the coconut on a baking sheet and toast in the oven for 6 to 7 minutes. Watch carefully, as coconut burns fairly easily. Let cool.

In a medium bowl, stir together the, cheese, pineapple, sugar, and coconut. Set aside.

To assemble: Butter one side of each slice of bread. Place 4 slices on your work surface, buttered side down. Distribute the pineapple-cheese mixture evenly over the 4 slices. Place the remaining 4 bread slices on top, buttered side up. Carefully cut off the crusts (Hawaiian bread can tear easily). This helps pinch the bread together to create a tight seal.

STOVETOP METHOD Heat a large nonstick skillet over medium heat for 2 minutes. Put the sandwiches in the skillet (in batches if necessary), cover, and cook for 1½ to 2 minutes, or until the undersides are golden brown and the cheese has begun to soften. Uncover, and turn the sandwiches with a spatula, pressing firmly to flatten them slightly. Cover and cook for 1 minute, or until the undersides are golden brown. Turn the sandwiches again, press with the spatula, and cook for 30 seconds, or until the cheese is soft and creamy. Let cool slightly before serving, garnished with extra pineapple.

SANDWICH MAKER METHOD Preheat the sandwich maker (if your machine has adjustable heat, set it to medium). Follow directions for sandwich assembly, and cook according to the manufacturer's instructions.

GAS GRILL METHOD Brush the grill rack with oil and preheat the grill to medium. Follow directions for sandwich assembly. Put the sandwiches on the grill and follow directions for the stovetop method.

MAKES 4 SANDWICHES

CHOCOLATE-HAZELNUT AND GOAT CHEESE MELT

You'll love how quickly this elegant and rich dessert sandwich can be made. My faithful recipe tester Annette says it's kind of like a chocolate-hazelnut cheesecake, only much simpler to make. Usually, it's important to press grilled cheese sandwiches with a spatula to flatten them, but with this one, it's important not to press it, or the filling can squirt out.

8 tablespoons (about ½ cup) Nutella (or other hazelnut-
    chocolate spread)
4 ounces fresh goat cheese, at room temperature
8 slices country white bread (¼ inch thick)
2 tablespoons butter, at room temperature

In a small bowl, stir the Nutella and cheese together.

To assemble: Butter one side of each slice of bread. Place 4 slices on your work surface, buttered side down. Spread the cheese mixture evenly over the 4 slices so that it is about ¼ inch thick (if it's any thicker, the sandwich will be too gooey). Place the remaining 4 bread slices on top, buttered side up. Cut off the crusts (this helps pinch the bread together to create a tight seal).

STOVETOP METHOD Heat a large nonstick skillet over medium heat for 2 minutes. Put the sandwiches in the skillet (in batches if necessary), cover, and cook for 2 minutes or until the undersides are golden brown and the cheese has begun to soften. Uncover, and turn the sandwiches with a spatula. Cook for 1 minute or until the undersides are golden brown. Turn the sandwiches again, and cook for 30 seconds, or until the cheese is soft and creamy. Serve immediately.

Because of the creaminess of the filling, a sandwich maker does not work for this sandwich.

Brush a grill rack with oil and preheat the grill to medium. Follow directions for sandwich assembly. Put the sandwiches on the grill and follow directions for the stovetop method.

MAKES 4 SANDWICHES

• • •

CREAMY CHOCOLATE AND PEAR

Though it may seem strange to combine cottage cheese and chocolate, all you have to do is make this rich grilled cheese once to find out how well they go together. The addition of the pear not only lends sweetness, but it also re-creates the flavor of one of the best-ever chocolate confections: chocolate-covered pears.

> 3 tablespoons unsalted butter, at room temperature
> 1 ripe but firm large pear (about 8 ounces) such as Anjou or Bosc, cut into ¼-inch-thick slices; slices cut into thirds crosswise
> 1 cup cottage cheese (lowfat is okay)
> 1 teaspoon sugar
> 2½ tablespoons chocolate chips
> 8 slices egg bread (¼ inch thick)

In a large nonstick skillet, melt 1 tablespoon of the butter over medium-high heat. Add the pears and cook until they are soft but not mushy, about 4 minutes. Transfer to a plate to cool. Wipe the skillet with a paper towel, but do not wash it.

In a small bowl, mix together the cottage cheese, sugar, and chocolate chips.

To assemble: Butter one side of each slice of bread with the remaining 2 tablespoons butter. Place 4 slices on your work surface, buttered side down. Distribute the cheese mixture evenly over the 4 slices, followed by the pears. Place the remaining 4 bread slices on top, buttered side up.

STOVETOP METHOD Heat the same skillet over medium heat for 2 minutes. Put the sandwiches in the skillet (in batches if necessary), cover, and cook for 2 minutes, or until the undersides are golden brown and the cheese has begun to soften. Uncover, and turn the sandwiches with a spatula, pressing firmly to flatten them slightly. Cover and cook for 1 to 2 minutes more, or until the undersides are golden brown. Turn the sandwiches again, press with the spatula, and cook for 30 seconds, or until the cheese is soft and creamy. Serve immediately.

SANDWICH MAKER METHOD Preheat the sandwich maker (if your sandwich maker has adjustable heat, set it to medium). Follow directions for sandwich assembly, and cook according to the manufacturer's instructions.

GAS GRILL METHOD Brush the grill rack with oil and preheat the grill to medium. Follow directions for sandwich assembly. Put the sandwiches on the grill and follow directions for the stovetop method.

MAKES 4 SANDWICHES

RICOTTA AND MARMALADE WITH CHOCOLATE SAUCE

The chocolate sauce helps elevate this grilled cheese sandwich to a downright elegant affair. Still, it is finger food, which makes for a casual dessert.

> 4 ounces semisweet chocolate, finely chopped
> ¼ cup plus 1 tablespoon whole milk or cream
> 1 cup ricotta cheese, at room temperature (drain if watery)
> ¼ cup orange marmalade
> 8 slices country white bread (¼ inch thick)
> 2 tablespoons unsalted butter, at room temperature

Place the chocolate in a medium-size heatproof bowl and set aside.

In a small saucepan, heat the milk over medium heat until just a few bubbles form. Pour the milk over the chocolate and stir until the pieces have melted. Transfer the mixture to a small serving bowl and set aside.

In a small bowl, mix the cheese and marmalade together. Set aside.

To assemble: Butter one side of each slice of bread. Place 4 slices on your work surface, buttered side down. Spread the cheese mixture evenly over the 4 slices. Place the remaining 4 bread slices on top, buttered side up.

STOVETOP METHOD Heat a large nonstick skillet over medium heat for 2 minutes. Put the sandwiches in the skillet (in batches if necessary), cover, and cook for 1 to 2 minutes, or until the undersides are golden brown and the cheese has begun to soften. Uncover, and turn the sandwiches with a spatula, pressing lightly to flatten them slightly. Cook for

1 to 2 minutes more, or until the undersides are golden brown. Turn the sandwiches again, and cook for 30 seconds, or until the cheese is soft and creamy.

To serve, cut in half diagonally. Spoon a little chocolate sauce onto individual plates or directly onto the sandwiches.

SANDWICH MAKER METHOD Preheat the sandwich maker (if your machine has adjustable heat, set it to medium). Follow directions for sandwich assembly, and cook according to the manufacturer's instructions. Lower the lid carefully; if too much weight is put on the sandwiches, the filling will ooze out.

GAS GRILL METHOD Brush the grill rack with oil and preheat the grill to medium-high. Follow directions for sandwich assembly. Put the sandwiches on the grill and follow directions for the stovetop method.

MAKES 4 SANDWICHES

RICH RASPBERRY BRIOCHE

Like many sweet grilled sandwiches, this one finds itself at home as an after-dinner sandwich or as a brunch-time treat. When you assemble the sandwich, make sure to position the raspberries in neat rows—it will look much prettier when you cut it.

8 ounces fresh goat cheese
2 tablespoons plus 2 teaspoons sugar
½ teaspoon lemon juice
2 tablespoons unsalted butter, at room temperature
8 slices brioche or egg bread (¼ inch thick)
½ pint raspberries (about 6 ounces), washed and dried well

In a small bowl, mix the cheese with 2 tablespoons of the sugar and the lemon juice. Set aside.

To assemble: Butter one side of each slice of bread with the butter, and sprinkle the remaining 2 teaspoons sugar over the buttered bread. Place 4 slices on your work surface, buttered side down. Spread the cheese mixture evenly over the 4 slices. Carefully position the raspberries in neat rows over the cheese. Place the remaining 4 bread slices on top, buttered side up. Cut off the crusts (this helps pinch the bread together to create a tight seal).

STOVETOP METHOD Heat a large nonstick skillet over medium heat for 2 minutes. Put the sandwiches in the skillet (in batches if necessary), cover, and cook for 2 minutes or until the undersides are golden brown and the cheese has begun to soften. Watch carefully, because the sugar burns fairly easily. Uncover, and turn the sandwiches, pressing each one *lightly* with a spatula to flatten them slightly. Cook for 1 minute or

until the undersides are golden brown. Turn the sandwiches again, press lightly with the spatula, and cook for 30 seconds, or until the cheese is soft and creamy. Serve immediately.

SANDWICH MAKER METHOD Preheat a sandwich maker (if your sandwich maker has adjustable heat, set it to medium). Follow directions for sandwich assembly, and cook according to the manufacturer's instructions.

GAS GRILL METHOD Brush a grill rack with oil and preheat the grill to medium. Follow directions for sandwich assembly. Put the sandwiches on the grill and follow directions for the stovetop method.

MAKES 4 SANDWICHES

GOAT CHEESE AND HONEY ON CINNAMON-RAISIN BREAD

innamon-raisin bread is a sweet treat, and the perfect complement to the tart goat cheese in this sandwich. The rich honey adds a welcome herbaceous note. Feel free to experiment with different types of honey to find your favorite flavor combination.

> 2 tablespoons unsalted butter, at room temperature
> 8 slices cinnamon-raisin bread (¼ inch thick)
> 4 ounces fresh goat cheese
> 2 teaspoons honey

To assemble: Butter one side of each slice of bread. Place 4 slices on your work surface, buttered side down. Spread the cheese evenly over the 4 slices, then drizzle with the honey. Place the remaining 4 bread slices on top, buttered side up. Cut the crusts off the bread (this helps pinch the bread together to create a nice seal).

STOVETOP METHOD Heat a large nonstick skillet over medium heat for 2 minutes. Put the sandwiches in the skillet (in batches if necessary), cover, and cook for 2 to 3 minutes, or until the undersides are golden brown and the cheese has begun to soften. Uncover, and turn the sandwiches with a spatula, pressing firmly to flatten them slightly. Cover and cook for 1 minute, or until the undersides are golden brown. Turn the sandwiches again, press with the spatula, and cook for 30 seconds, or until the cheese is soft and creamy. Serve immediately.

SANDWICH MAKER METHOD Preheat the sandwich maker (if it has adjustable heat, set it to medium). Follow directions for sandwich assembly, and cook according to the manufacturer's instructions.

GAS GRILL METHOD Brush the grill rack with oil and preheat the grill to medium-high. Follow directions for sandwich assembly. Put the sandwiches on the grill and follow directions for the stovetop method.

MAKES 4 SANDWICHES

• • •

NECTARINES, BLUEBERRIES, AND RICOTTA ON EGG BREAD

This sandwich could easily be called "grilled summertime," for it showcases the best of the warm months in the form of juicy stone fruits and berries nestled in creamy ricotta. Although this recipe calls for nectarines, it works equally well with peaches. Just be sure to skin them first.

8 ounces ricotta cheese, at room temperature (drain if watery)
1 large nectarine (about 1 pound), cut into ¼-inch slices
6 tablespoons blueberries
1 tablespoon plus 1 teaspoon sugar
½ teaspoon cinnamon
8 slices egg bread (¼ inch thick)
2 tablespoons unsalted butter, at room temperature
Confectioners' sugar for dusting

In a small bowl, stir together the cheese, fruit, sugar, and cinnamon. Set aside.

To assemble: Butter one side of each slice of bread. Place 4 slices on your work surface, buttered side down. Distribute the cheese mixture evenly over the 4 slices. Place the remaining 4 bread slices on top, buttered side up. Cut off the crusts (this helps pinch the bread together to create a tight seal).

STOVETOP METHOD Heat a large nonstick skillet over medium heat for 2 minutes. Put the sandwiches in the skillet (in batches if necessary), cover, and cook for 2 minutes, or until the undersides are golden brown and the cheese has begun to soften. Uncover, and turn the sandwiches with a spatula, pressing firmly to flatten them slightly. Cook for 1 minute, or until the undersides are golden brown. Turn the sandwiches again, press with the spatula, and cook for 30 seconds, or until the cheese is soft and creamy. Remove from the skillet and let cool for 3 to 5 minutes. Sprinkle generously with confectioners' sugar and serve immediately.

SANDWICH MAKER METHOD Preheat the sandwich maker (if your machine has adjustable heat, set it to medium). Follow directions for sandwich assembly, and cook according to the manufacturer's instructions.

GAS GRILL METHOD Brush the grill rack with oil and preheat the grill to medium. Follow directions for sandwich assembly. Put the sandwiches on the grill and follow directions for the stovetop method.

MAKES 4 SANDWICHES

INDEX